The Ultimate Guide to Podcasting
Jamie Bunting & Aaron Fisher

© Copyright, MunchTech.TV

All rights reserved. No part of this work may be reproduced or transmitted in any form or by any means, electrical or mechanical, including photocopying, recording or by any information storage or retrieval system, without prior written permission of the copyright owner.

Copyright © 2012. All rights reserved.

Trademarked names may appear in this book. These names are not symbolised by the registered trademark symbol ™, but instead are used in an editorial fashion and to benefit the trademark owner, with no intention of infringement.

Reference herein to any specific commercial products, process, or service by trade name, trademark, manufacturer, or otherwise, does not constitute or imply its endorsement by MunchTech, PodcastAssist or the authors. All products, services and processes mentioned herein are personal recommendations from the authors, and are not sponsored nor endorsed in any way.

Information herein is accurate to the best of the authors knowledge as of the time of writing and publishing.

All images are property of rightful owner.

ISBN: 978-1-291-32507-2

Authors
Jamie Bunting
Aaron Fisher

MunchTech.TV is licensed under a Creative Commons Attribution-NonCommercial-NoDerivs 3.0 Unported License.
Based on work at munchtech.tv and podcastassist.com

Permissions beyond the scope of this license may be available at munchtech.tv and podcastassist.com

Contents
at a glance

Chapter 1: Introduction	4
Chapter 2: Fundamentals	6
Chapter 3: Identifying Your Show	9
Chapter 4: Microphones	11
Chapter 5: Mixers	15
Chapter 6: Headphones	20
Chapter 7: Compressors	21
Chapter 8: Cameras	24
Chapter 9: Capture Cards	25
Chapter 10: Cables	26
Chapter 11: Show Preparation	27
Chapter 12: Recording	31
Chapter 13: Broadcasting Live	39
Chapter 14: Editing	44
Chapter 15: Hosting	50
Chapter 16: Podcast Website	54
Chapter 17: Distribution	67
Chapter 18: Tracking Statistics	70
Chapter 19: Promotion	74
Chapter 20: Monetisation	80
Chapter 21: Podcasting for Businesses	85
Chapter 22: The Future	90
Glossary	92
Cheat Sheet	93

Introduction

Chapter Summary

In this chapter we'll introduce you to podcasting, why you may want to start your own podcast and the advantages of doing so.

This textbook encloses all of the information needed to start your own podcast, without making the mistakes that many commonly make, helping you get it right, the first time!

Summary

From the folks at MunchTech, a leading online podcast network and PodcastAssist, this book covers everything that you need to know about starting your own podcast. No assumptions are made, so even if you don't know what a podcast is, by the end of this book you'll be able to produce your own podcast and reach out to thousands around the world!

What's Covered?

This textbook goes from the very beginning of creating your own podcast to getting a name, choosing what you're going to talk about, helping you decide what equipment is best and to buy, recording, editing, publishing as well as promoting and monetizing your podcast.

About Podcasting

Look up in a dictionary, the word 'podcast' - you'll find something along the lines of "A multimedia digital file made available on the Internet for downloading to a portable media player, computer, etc." A podcast is much more, it's a way to communicate with the world, to express your thoughts, as well as join the vast expanding digital media world; and put your mark on the table.

When starting a podcast, many people turn to the Internet for information, however; not many sites go into much detail and if they do, it's normally on one specific part of podcasting. This textbook, encloses that information to allow you to read up on specific parts of podcasting, and/or learn everything you need to start your own.

This book is great for anyone who wants to either start their own podcast, have already started one but want help on some aspects of podcasting or even people who have been podcasting for quite some time but want to learn more about it in general, improve their show or learn more about specific parts of podcasting.

Podcasting is a fairly new form of media compared to others, and puts the power of your own 'radio or television show' into your own hands. Making your podcast stand out will be key in making it a successful one, and there are many ways to do that! But ultimately, success is what you make it - and making a show that people enjoy, is success in itself.

Did you know?

The name "Podcast" is a combination of "broadcast" and "iPod" - the name was taken due to the success of the iPod, and so a new medium was created.

Introduction

Power of Podcasting

In October 2011 Apple inc. announced that they had sold more than 300 million iPods, and that number is ever increasing! You're probably asking yourself what relevance this has to podcasting, well; iTunes! Every iPod has the ability to play podcasts and uses the iTunes store to search for podcasts, where your potential show will be!

Price of Podcasting

Radio stations spend thousands of pounds/dollars on equipping their studios out with microphones, headphones, computers, highly complex telephone lines, transmitters etc. All of this equipment doesn't come cheap, so, you'll be happy to know that you don't even need a fraction of that to start your own show! We'll take a look at that in "equipment".

What's in it For You?

Podcasting is a fantastic way to get your thoughts out there! Many people who share the same interests as you are interested in what others (including you) have to say about that topic, and that's were podcasts come in! Podcasts can range from literally hundreds of topics; technology, cars, home theatre, sports, DIY, teaching, parenting, having a better lifestyle, cooking, medical topics, TV shows and careers just to list a few.

You can also have people on your podcast to help balance the discussion, and mix things up but that's only if you want! You can ask your listeners/viewers to email you with their opinions and read it on your podcast and maybe discuss why you agree, or even disagree! Podcasting is extremely versatile and that's why it's so popular among many communities.

Throughout this book, we'll cover everything you need about starting your own show. So, what are you waiting for? Lets get started

Fundamentals

> **Chapter Summary**
>
> The fundamentals of your podcasts act as the foundation, or roots of your show.
>
> Things such as what you're going to talk about, the duration of your show, release schedule etc. are all considered the fundamentals of your show - and obviously build the main parts of your podcast.

Summary

The fundamentals of your podcast are important to establish ground on what you're going to talk about, how long your show's going to last, when you're going to release a new episode, the format of your show etc.

What You're Going to Talk About

The topic of your show is an important choice to make, it decides who listens to your show. An important fact to remember is that you should podcast about something you're interested in, and are passionate about. It's completely up to you, but if you're not interested in the topic you're podcasting on, it'll certainly show and will drive your audience away from your podcast due to your lack of interest. Not only that, but if you're podcasting about something you enjoy doing, or something you're passionate about, the odds are you'll have a lot of knowledge about it and so your show becomes a lot more interesting due to this alone! Your knowledge will show you have an interest in that topic and will keep listeners engaged as they're enjoying the show and are learning something new!

No matter what your podcast is going to be about, there will be people who are interested - so even if you are unsure as to whether you should podcast on a particular topic as you don't share the interest with millions - don't let that put you off! There will be people online who do share the same interest/hobby as you and will be intrigued in your show!

The more topic specific your show is, the smaller the market you are going to reach out to. However, don't let this put you off choosing a niche topic, sometimes these topics are not covered by anyone and so people will naturally find your show because it is the only one out discussing that particular subject. Just keep in mind, the more general your show, the higher percentage of the market you will reach out to and vice versa. Having a show that is too vague can also be detrimental. You want to find a happy medium between not specific enough and too specific.

Did you know?

It is estimated that there are more than 150,000 podcasts available online as of 2011 - and that number is constantly increasing!

Fundamentals   7

Duration of Your Show

The duration of your show is yet another important decision you have to make. Both short and long shows have their advantages and disadvantages. The majority of podcasts range from 10 minutes to an hour. Short podcasts can be more popular among people simply due to the fact that they're short, the content is easy to "consume" and they get the point across quickly. However; just because your show is short doesn't mean that it's including all of the information you want it to. 30 Minute shows allow room for more discussion, meet the happy medium between short and long and mean you can extend your conversation for longer. Hour long shows allow you to include a lot more detail - but you have to have enough content; you don't want to carry a story out longer than it should be, otherwise you'll just be rambling on, which will make the show boring.

Sticking to a strict schedule isn't always possible, so it's not a huge deal if you're under or over by 10 - 15 minutes, but when your show normally lasts 45 minutes and your latest show only lasts 10, it can get annoying for your listeners. Occasionally this happens, and that's fine, but try not to make it an often occurrence. Also, when considering duration; think about your schedule. If you're recording and releasing every day you're probably not going to want to record and release an hour long show. You probably won't have the time for it, and your listeners certainly won't have the time to listen! If you're recording and releasing once every week however, this is perfect! It means your listeners don't have too much to listen to, and they have an extended period of time to listen to it and as a result, not "backlogging" them with content, which could lead to them unsubscribing.

When You're Going to Record and Release

The next factor you have to consider is when you're going to record and release your show. Your release schedule is like the heartbeat of your show. It should be consistent and shouldn't change every episode. Most shows are weekly, some are daily and some are even biweekly (every two weeks). The majority though, are weekly. This meets the happy medium and doesn't "overflow" your audience with content to listen to. Remember, your show probably isn't the only one that your audience are subscribed to. As mentioned in the previous section, when considering the release schedule of your podcast take into consideration the duration of your show! Your listeners want consistency, so when you're deciding when you're going to record and release your show make sure you're normally free at that time, whether that's on a weekend, a day off, at night or in the morning. The same goes for when you release your show - keep it constant! Your listeners will get to know your schedule and will look out for new releases. If you talk about any type of news, or developments in the topic your podcast is based on, make the time between recording and releasing as minimal as possible - simply because the news will change and it won't wait up for you which will make your show's information irrelevant. In other words, if the topic you're talking about is "time sensitive" make sure to release it soon after recording.

Fundamentals 8

Format of Your Show

The format is basically how your show is going to run. Over time and episodes your show will develop it's own format, and will become unique in style. Consider how you're going to present your show - at the beginning are you going to "tease" your audience with what you're going to be talking about. Try to have your audience intrigued by what you say so that they listen attentively. Also, make sure your show is of excellent quality from the second you begin to the second you end. This is important as people who are discovering your show will play it and will skip to certain sections, and if that one part they hear isn't of good quality, they'll quickly click off your show.

Also, consider doing a "run down" at the start of your show on what you're going to talk about on the episode. Or, are you just going to "surprise" your audience?

It's entirely up to yourself on how you present and format your show - try to do what you feel works best with the topic of your show.

You can also ask your audience to email you questions and/or feedback and in return you'll read it aloud on the show, or at least some of it. This is great, as it gives a sense of interaction between you and your audience.

What ever style and format you choose, make sure to entice your audience; experiment with your style; sooner rather than later you'll be confident with your presenting and format and your audience will love it! Once again, make sure the topic(s) you're talking about are intriguing not only to your audience, but to you as well! If you're not interested in the topic, soon they won't be interested in the show.

Identifying Your Show   9

Chapter Summary

Your show is identified by numerous factors, such as it's name, artwork and jingles. These are unique to your show and will help both potential listeners and listeners to identify your show from the crowd.

We'll take a look at these factors, explain why they're important, why good quality artwork is needed and why your show name matters.

Summary

Your show is one in thousands, and it has to be separated from the crowd! Otherwise, why will people chose your show instead of someone else's? These factors will help insure your show stands out from the crowd and will help give great initial impressions of your show. When people are searching for podcasts they're not going to decide whether or not to subscribe by listening to your show, instead they're going to look for the best name and artwork.

Naming Your Show

Your show's name is unique to your podcast! It's the very first thing people see when they find your show. Thinking of a name can be the hardest part of creating your show. Many times, a perfect name comes to mind only to find it's already taken! Try to be original and creative when thinking of your name. Often, complex or over-complicated names are a bad idea, as people are not searching for them and your show will be pushed to the bottom, if listed at all.

For example, if you're starting a show about car news; you could use a basic name such as "Car News Weekly" and it would be high up when people search for "cars" in iTunes, Zune and other podcast directories. However, if you decide to go with a complex name, like "Speed Machine" - it is more than likely that it will be ranked lower than "Car News Weekly". Of course, the name may sound better, but it may not be as high up in the rankings. Try to find the happy medium between to basic to sound good and too advanced to be listed. If you're familiar with SEO (Search Engine Optimisation) then you'll probably understand this concept better. It's also recommended not to use abbreviations in your name if it can be avoided as they're difficult to remember and don't clearly represent your show's purpose.

Show Artwork

Next, is artwork. Now your show has a name, you're in with the thousands of other podcasts that are like yours. What makes yours stand out from the crowd to potential subscribers? Aesthetics. Artwork is extremely important, it gives your show the professional look, if done right. If not, you'll lose potential subscribers and will give your podcast the a bad image.

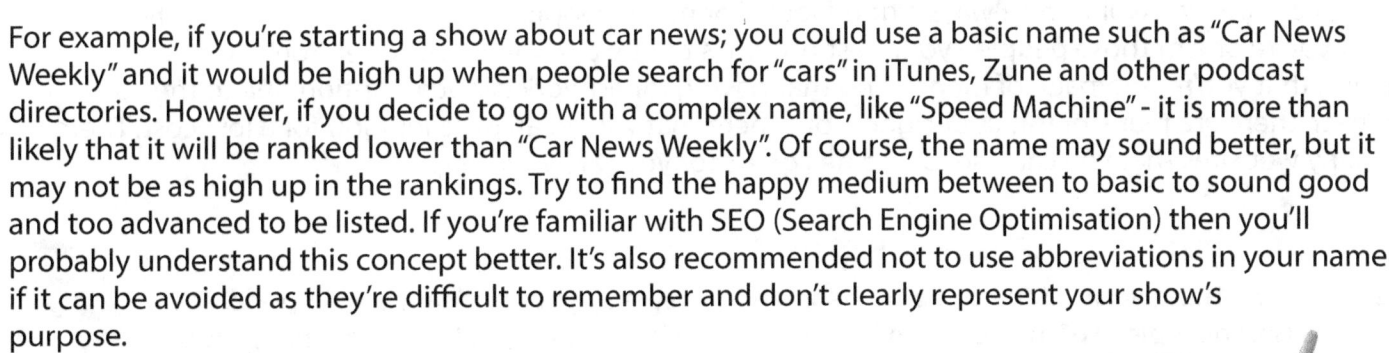

Identifying Your Show

You don't want to overcomplicate your artwork, but you don't want to have basic artwork either. Finding the happy medium is key. Below, on the right, is the real artwork for one of our shows (The Two Techies) - and a very rough and quick mockup of terrible artwork, on the left. You can probably see for yourself why good artwork is extremely important for your podcast.

People do judge books by their cover, aesthetics can be everything or nothing in certain cases. It's the same with everything; if you have two cars that have the same features and functions, but one looks a lot nicer than the other - you can guess which one you're going to choose. When you're deciding on your artwork, ask yourself "would I subscribe to that if I saw it on iTunes, or online?" If the answer is no, then you obviously need to make amendments.

Making your own artwork isn't always a good idea. For many people, they just don't know where to start. If you're one of those people - your best option is to hire a graphics designer. You're probably now thinking that you're not made of money and that paying for artwork is not an option due to the cost! However, there are many graphics designers out there that will do an excellent job for a low cost. There are many websites that you can use to find designers for your artwork.

Your Intro/Outro Jingles

One of the first thing your listeners should hear when they play your podcast is your podcast's intro. This is a short piece of music which identifies your show. Good jingles will definitely add to the production value of your podcast. One thing you definitely don't want to do is use real, copyrighted music, for obvious reasons. There are many sites online that sell "production music" (music safe for broadcasts) for £20-40. It's just finding the right sites. There are also sites that charge thousands for production music and libraries, those you'll probably not be interested in. There are also a few free alternatives that can work just as well. If you have a Mac and GarageBand which is included in the iLife package, you can use the loops that come with GarageBand for your podcast intro and outro. Your intro and outro can be important for establishing the tone of your podcast, for example; if your podcast is very upbeat and lively you will more than likely want music to match that tone. But you can also choose a different tone of music, it's completely up to yourself!

Microphones   11

Chapter Summary

In this chapter, we'll take a look at the different types of microphones, explain what a microphone pattern is, why choosing the right one is important amongst other things.

Many people believe to achieve great audio, you need to spend hundreds, if not thousands on good quality microphones. However, with wise decision making and careful consideration you can buy an excellent microphone for much less.

Summary

Microphones are an obvious piece of equipment, that without - you can't make a podcast. The common myth about microphones is that you have to spend a lot of money to get a good sounding one, and while more expensive microphones will sound generally better, you can still find an amazing sounding microphone for a low price.

Different Types of Microphone

All microphones are the same, right? Wrong! There are a few different types of microphones, and understanding the differences between each one will help you in choosing the right one. There are also microphone 'patterns' which decipher the area from which a microphone picks noise from which we'll also look at.

Types of Microphone

Condenser Microphones - Condenser microphones tend to have a better 'frequency response', which basically respond better to more noise tones and are more sensitive to noise. If you're recording in a noisy environment these aren't always ideal as they pick up a lot of background noise. For example, if you have a fan on in the background the noise, and possible wind produced by the fan will be picked up and will cause irritation to your listeners. Condenser microphones also require external power, otherwise known as phantom power. If you decide to use a condenser microphone, make sure the mixer you decide to purchase supports it, condenser microphone's use phantom power to both power the circuitry and polarise the microphone's transducer element.

Dynamic Microphones - These are less responsive to noise around you and require you to speak closer to the microphone. Dynamic microphones tend to be better for podcasts as they filter out some of the unwanted noise that will distract your listeners. They do take a bit of getting used to due to their sensitive nature, however - you soon learn the 'technique' which is basically to keep your mouth to the front of the microphone at all times and not move your head from side to side unless you are moving the microphone as you're moving your mouth. There are other types of microphone such as the ribbon microphone and although they produce a very warm and rich sound, they are very delicate and are easily broken, thus they are becoming quite rare, and used less and less.

Did you know?

The first microphone ever invented was a a telephone transmitter, invented by Emile Berliner for Alexander Graham Bell, in 1876!

Microphones   12

Polar Patterns

Also known as 'pickup patterns', polar patterns are the areas of which a microphone picks up audio/noise. The 'tighter' the pickup pattern, the smaller the area the microphone takes in audio from.

There are quite a few different types of pickup patterns, we'll take a look at the main ones.

Cardioid - The cardioid pattern rejects audio from the back of the microphone. It follows (as pictured on the diagram) the pattern of a heart. Audio is picked up from the front and the side. A cardioid pattern is good for podcasts due to the fact that it doesn't let unwanted noise through; such as computer fans or other noise within the room. There are also 'super-cardioid' and 'hyper-cardioid' patterns that follow the same basic principle, but have tighter pickup patterns and so exaggerate the pattern of a cardioid microphone.

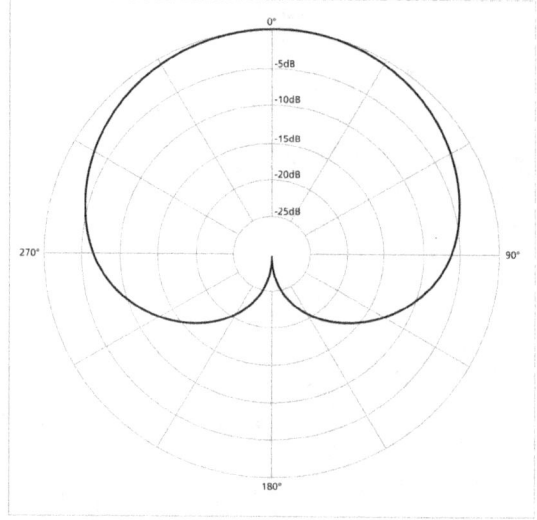

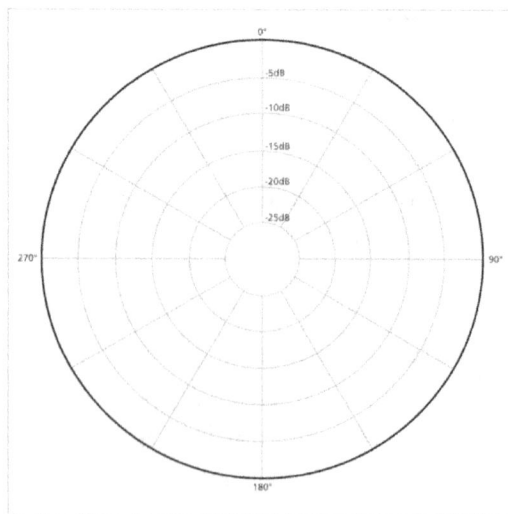

Omnidirectional - Omnidirectional patterns are pretty self explanatory. They pick up sound from every angle, for the majority of setups it's not the best option as with podcasts - when you're in a noisy environment or only have one person talking. Even if more than one person is talking, it's more than often unideal.

Others - There are other polar patterns such as bi-directional and shotgun patterns, however; these are not normally used for radio or podcast setups.

Generally, the cardioid and omnidirectional patterns are more common in studio type setups, which ever one you get is ultimately up to you - however, it's recommended that you go for a cardioid pattern due to the reasons we looked at.

Microphones   13

XLR & USB

The next thing you need to consider is whether or not to buy a USB or XLR microphone. This decision is a simpler one. In summary, USB is digital from the microphone to the computer and doesn't require an 'interface' (such as a mixer or audio interface) to connect to your computer, whereas XLR does. USB microphones tend to be cheaper, though have less "flexibility".

XLR microphones tend to cost more than USB ones, and require an audio interface/mixer (see diagram below). However, as mentioned before, have more flexibility. This allows you to modify the volume and gain easily, as well as adding equalisation to your audio to modify the sound. For many beginners, the best option is to start off with a USB microphone and work your way up. Not only because it is the cheapest option, but also because it is the only thing you need, along with a computer and some software.

Whatever type of connection you decide to go with, is completely up to you. As a general rule, USB microphones are cheaper although don't allow you to modify the sound as easily, and vice versa for XLR microphones. Below is a list of recommended microphones, both XLR and USB.

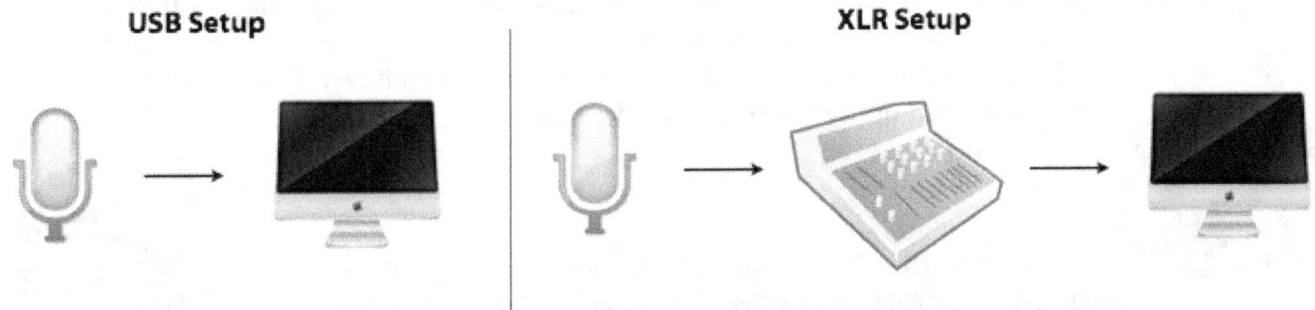

USB	XLR
Samsung Go Mic - Condenser Microphone	Shure SM58 - Dynamic Microphone
Blue Snowball - Condenser Microphone	Rode Procaster - Dynamic Microphone
Samsung CO1U - Condenser Microphone	Heil PR40 - Dynamic Microphone
Rode Podcaster - Dynamic Microphone	Electrovoice RE20 - Dynamic Microphone

Choosing the right microphone is important, and quite a few factors come into play when deciding on this. However, with the information above, you should hopefully be able to make an informed decision on what to buy and what's best for you.

Microphones   14

Microphone Accessories

Now that you've decided what type of microphone you're going to buy and use for your podcast - you need to decide what type of stand to use. Although not essential, a stand will surely save you from an aching arm because of holding the microphone, which is less than ideal. There are various types of stands with various price ranges. We'll take a look at the main ones.

Angle-poise Stand - Angle-poise stands are commonly used in radio studios, along with home studios as they save a lot of space, and allow 360 degrees rotation of the stand, in whatever shape is comfortable, allowing you to move the microphone to a position that suits you, instead of you having to move or lean over to speak into the microphone. Due to these factors, they don't exactly come cheap with most costing around $145 (£90). However, you can find non-branded ones online for less if you look around. Two common ones being the "Rode PSA1" and the "Heil PL-2T".

Desk Stand - Desk Stand's are considerably cheaper than angle-poise stands. Many only costing around $15 (£9) or less! Although they are very basic compared to the other, they still get the job done and well! They can make things awkward when it comes to positioning the microphone and yourself to find a comfortable position for both - but for the price, you can't complain! One disadvantage to this type of stand is that you can accidentally hit the microphone with your hand/arm if it is in the way - which will be picked up by the microphone and will be heard in the recording.

Shock mount - Shock mount's are used to keep your microphone isolated from stand/desk vibrations that would otherwise be picked up, and heard on recordings. Many microphones have specific types of shock mounts that fit them precisely. Depending on the make of microphone you have, the price of shock mounts change drastically.

Although they're not completely necessary - shock mounts can prevent loud "thumps" coming through on your audio.

Pop filter - Pop filters and Windshields are useful to prevent loud 'popping' sounds that are caused by fast moving air on the microphone while talking. The popping sound generally occurs in the pronunciation of plosives (such as the letter "p", "b" and "t").

Mixers   15

Chapter Summary

In this chapter, we'll take a look at the different types of mixers and look at why they can make the workflow of your podcast a lot easier.

There are many different types of mixers, and many different ones for different reasons. We'll take a look at them, and explain when/where they'll come in handy. Along with some recommended mixers that you may find suit what you want/need.

Summary

Mixers, although not *always* needed - can make editing and mixing multiple streams of audio into one much easier than what it would be in software. They allow for live editing while recording your podcast.

Types of Mixers

Different types of mixers are used for different types of uses and applications. There are two main categories of mixers that are popular in the audio field. We'll also explain the different functions and features of mixers.

Analogue vs. Digital

The two main different types of mixers are analogue and digital. Both have their advantages and disadvantages.

Analogue mixers combine signals using analogue techniques. On an analogue mixer, each of several inputs, for microphones or other inputs feed into a master amplifier. The master amplifier also has a fader that controls the overall loudness. These sounds are combined, routed and modified as an electrical signal.

Digital mixers take each sound signal input and convert it into a rapid stream of numbers. This is called analogue to digital conversion (ADC). The mixer combines, routes and processes the numbers with computer software. At it's output, the digital mixer converts the numeric information back to standard electrical signals, this is known as digital to analogue conversion (DAC). Digital mixers have many of the physical features of analogue models, including faders, dials and switches; but internally the circuits are very different.

Right For You

For podcasting, an analogue mixer is an obvious choice, digital mixers are completely unnecessary and are extremely expensive, costing thousands of dollars, compared to analogue equivalents, which you can get for under $100.

Did you know?

Mixing consoles started out in 1950's as purely analogue devices with only one or two channels.

Mixers   16

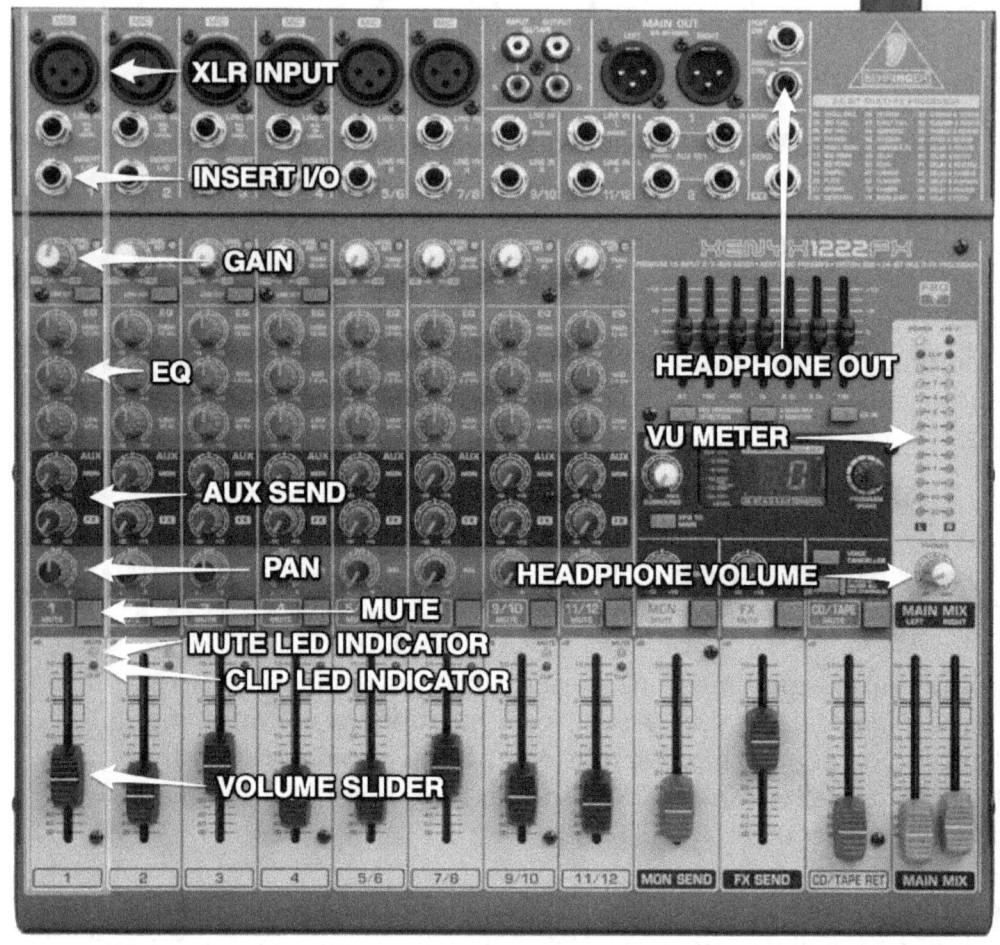

What's That?

At first glance, a mixer can seem extremely complicated and intimidating. However, they're definitely not!

Most people look at all of the dials, sliders and inputs and don't know where to start.

The first thing to understand is that one channel is repeated, and so - if you understand the buttons on one channel, you understand all of them! If you look to the very left of the diagram, you'll see a yellow rectangle highlighting a portion of the mixer. This is known as a channel 'strip'. These strips are repeated for each channel. And thus have separate controls for each; which is why there are so many buttons, dials and sliders. The same layout is just repeated for every channel! The diagram above is labelled - and below is a glossary of what the function of the button/slider is.

XLR Input - This is where your XLR cable will plug into, to connect your microphone (or any other XLR input) to your mixer. When purchasing an XLR cable for your microphone (if it doesn't come with one supplied), you'll want to purchase a 'male to female' XLR cable.

Insert I/O - The Insert I/O stands for Insert In/Out. Simply put, it allows you to add peripherals to your mixer, such as compressors, equalisers and other advanced equipment which we'll cover later in the book.

Gain - Gain is used for amplifying the signal that is being sent from the input, in this case the audio is coming from the microphone. To set your gain, firstly set your volume slider to, or slightly above "0". Speak into your microphone and start to turn the gain dial up slowly. When you see two to three green bars light up on the 'VU Meter' while you're talking - stop. Then speak louder, if you see the VU Meter lights go into the red, then turn the dial down slightly.

Mixers

EQ - EQ is used to filter out tones/frequencies to help get a better sound on your microphone. Each microphone will have it's own 'sweet spot' for the EQ; so there is no specific way of setting this. Depending on your mixer, you may have two, three or even four options under EQ. Some/all of them may include high, medium, a frequency dial for medium and low. On most mid-range mixers you'll just have high, medium and low. When adjusting the EQ, many people turn the low up too much to get a richer sound to your audio, however; this won't give the desired result and instead will make your audio muffled and very unclear. Instead, make slight adjustments to your EQ until you get it right. Again, there are no specific settings for EQ and it does depend on the microphone you're using as well as what mixer you're using - but finding the right combination shouldn't take too long and will get you a good sound to your microphone.

Aux Send - Not all mixers come with aux send, and it's not always necessary - however, if you're planning on having people on your podcast via VOIP software such as Skype - this definitely makes the task less strenuous. Aux Send comes in useful when you want to setup 'Aux Return', however; if you're new to a mixer (which we'll assume you are) - then it's best that you learn everything about a mixer before you go into detail about it. We'll cover it later in the textbook.

Pan - Pan allows you to make a mono signal such as a microphone appear on the stereo output and position the source.

Mute - This allows you to mute the input from that specific channel.

Mute LED Indicator - This light will turn on when the mute button is pressed down (activated)

Clip LED Indicator - Clipping occurs when an amplifier is delivering more current to a speaker than it is capable of doing. Clipping basically clips or cuts off parts of the sound that it's trying to reproduce. Clipping distorts the audio, so you'll want to keep this light off.

Volume Slider - The volume slider is what it sounds like (no pun intended), it allows you to turn your audio volume up and down as it's being moved up and down. Normally, your volume slider should be set at or just slightly above '0'. If your audio doesn't sound loud enough at '0', tweak your gain dial; which we covered in the gain explanation in the previous page.

Headphone Output - This is a connection that is used to plug headphones into the mixer to allow you to monitor all of the audio that is being sent to the mixer, and being outputted.

VU (Volume Unit) Meter - The VU Meter is a very simple audio metering/monitoring device. It's designed to visually measure the volume of an audio signal, in this case the signal being sent to the output of the mixer. Typically, when sending audio to your mixer the VU meter should light up in or around '0'. If the lights go into the orange/red, you'll want to turn the volume of your input down.

Headphone Volume - This dial allows you to control the volume of your headphones plugged into your mixer.

Mixers   18

Main Output Slider - This slider allows you to control the overall volume of the output of the mixer.

Main Output - These are your main output connections, in this case; an XLR cable can be used to send the main output to a computer or digital recorder. However, more often than not the main out will be a 1/4" audio cable, and not an XLR one. If you're not familiar with common audio cables you will be by the end of the book, as we cover them later on.

So now you know the basic buttons and dials on a mixer, taking into account that different mixers may not have some listed above, or may have a slightly different layout. Some also have dials, instead of sliders for volume control.

What Do I Buy?

The type of mixer you buy is something that has multiple factors to take into consideration. Such as "are you going to have many inputs?" (such as microphones, computers, Skype and other inputs).

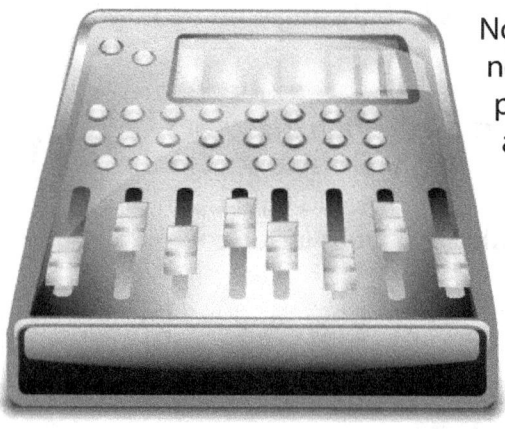

Normally, an 8-10 channel mixer will be more than enough for normal podcasts. You don't need to spend a lot of money to start a podcast - however, if it's something that you would really like to do, a mixer such as the "Behringer Xenyx 1204" will be more than enough for most situations. It's a 12 channel mixer with many features to suit what you'll need to start your own podcast. If you've decided to buy a USB microphone, you do not need a mixer - it's not that it's not necessary, but they're not compatible with mixers because of their input. Nor do they need a mixer to transfer the input to a computer.

Mixers

Summary

A mixer allows you to mix different inputs together, so if you have a microphone plugged into one channel, a Skype input in another and another for your music and jingles, you can mix all of these together without having to do it all in editing software.

Analogue mixers are more commonly found in podcast studios, mainly due to the price - digital mixers add some more complex, and mostly unnecessary features for average podcasters such as the ability to edit each track from one recording, however; this is normally not needed if you're monitoring your audio through headphones while recording.

Analogue mixers also give you more for less money, especially in terms of microphone preamps. Good sounding preamps are very important for good audio from your microphone. The majority of Behringer and Mackie mixers have high quality preamps built into them.

It's completely up to you on what type of mixer you buy - however, analogue mixers are a lot more common and cost a lot less money than digital mixers. For podcasting, analogue is more than enough for everything you'll need.

Noise

Analogue circuits must be carefully designed and used to avoid noise. All circuits create a small amount of hiss that creeps into the sound. More analogue circuitry means more chances for noise to build up. They can also pick up electrical interference from computers, mobile/cell phones and other sources. Digital circuits are less susceptible to this kind of noise, as signals are handled as numbers within the mixer.

If you ever hear any interference or noise in your audio that sounds unusual, the odds are other electrical equipment or cables are getting "caught up" with your audio cables. It's important to isolate these cables as they can cause what is known as "mains hum, electric hum or power line hum". When wiring your mixer, make sure your audio cables and electric cables are not near each other and are separated.

Headphones

20

Chapter Summary

In this chapter, we'll take a look at the different types of headphones, and why buying a decent pair can be important.

To you, headphones may just be something to listen to music - and that each pair is the same, apart from different makes. However, surprisingly - there are different types for different scenarios.

Summary

Headphones are used to monitor your audio while you are recording your podcast. It is important to make sure that your volume levels are correct during recording, and that you can be heard clearly. If not, you may have a hard time trying to correct your audio in editing, and you may not be able to completely correct it, especially if you were too loud and ended up distorted.

Types of Headphones

In podcasting - the trend is that there are multiple choices for hardware and software, and headphones are no different! There are different types of headphones, which have their advantages and disadvantages for different scenarios.

Open - "Open" headphones allow outside noise to pass through them, thus allowing you to hear audio not only from the headphones, but also audio from the room you're in. For recording, this can cause problems; especially if you're using a sensitive microphone and you've got the headphones turned up loud. For studio purposes, open headphones work, but aren't as ideal as other types.

Semi-open - "Semi-open" headphones aren't completely open, but aren't completely closed either - somewhere in between. They let some ambient noise through, but don't leak audio from the actual headphone as much, as a result, causing less feedback.

Closed - For studio purposes, "closed" headphones are the most convenient and less troublesome. Not only do they not allow ambient noise through, but they don't let a lot of noise out either unless you have them turned up quite loud; thus causing little to no feedback.

You don't have to spend a lot of money to find a good pair of headphones, anything around $20-30 is perfectly fine!

Did you know?

It is said to be that wearing headphones for an hour can increase the bacteria in your ear by up to 700 times!

Compressors

Chapter Summary

In this chapter, we'll take a look at the role of a compressor, why they can play a vital role in your podcast and what can happen without one.

Although hardware is the most common type of compressor - software compressors are as equally useful and serve the same purpose as hardware.

Summary

Compressors can play a vital role in your podcast, simply put, they keep your audio levels constant and stop them from fluctuating. This is important as if you move your head while speaking into your microphone while talking, your levels will go down and when you move closer to the microphone they will go back up, which will cause a lot of annoyance to your listeners.

Purpose of a Compressor

Compressors all serve the same purpose - they keep audio at a constant rate, but there are different types, ones with one/two channels and ones with three/four, even more channels. The amount of channels you need is decided by how many pieces of equipment you want to connect to the mixer.

Technically put, compressors and "limiters" are specialised amplifiers used to reduce "dynamic range". Dynamic range is the span between the softest and loudest sounds.

An Example of Compression

Below are waveforms of an identical audio recording, the only difference being compression has been applied to the audio in the second picture.

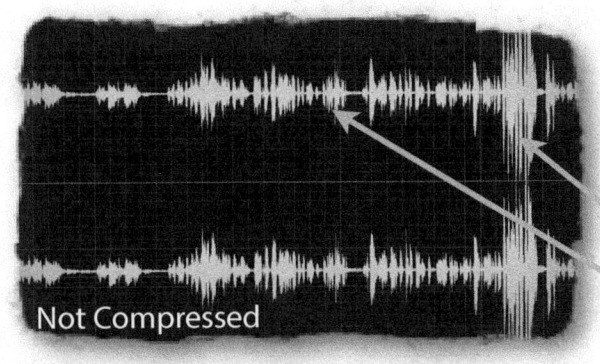

As you can see in the first waveform, there are peaks where the audio volume has increased. Peaks can occur when you talk louder/shout in the microphone, or simply when the volume suddenly changes in the audio.

Peak

Normal Volume

In the second waveform, the audio is level and constant as it has been compressed, and there are no obvious peaks.

Compressors

22

Setting up a Compressor

Compressors can seem difficult and confusing, but they couldn't be anything further from the truth. They are simple to setup, and offer great results. In this section, we'll take a look at setting compressors up and what the dials on the compressor actually do.

Below is a cutout of a mixer with an 'Insert I/O' port and the back of a compressor, for most setups, each channel on the mixer you wish to compress, you will use one channel on the compressor.

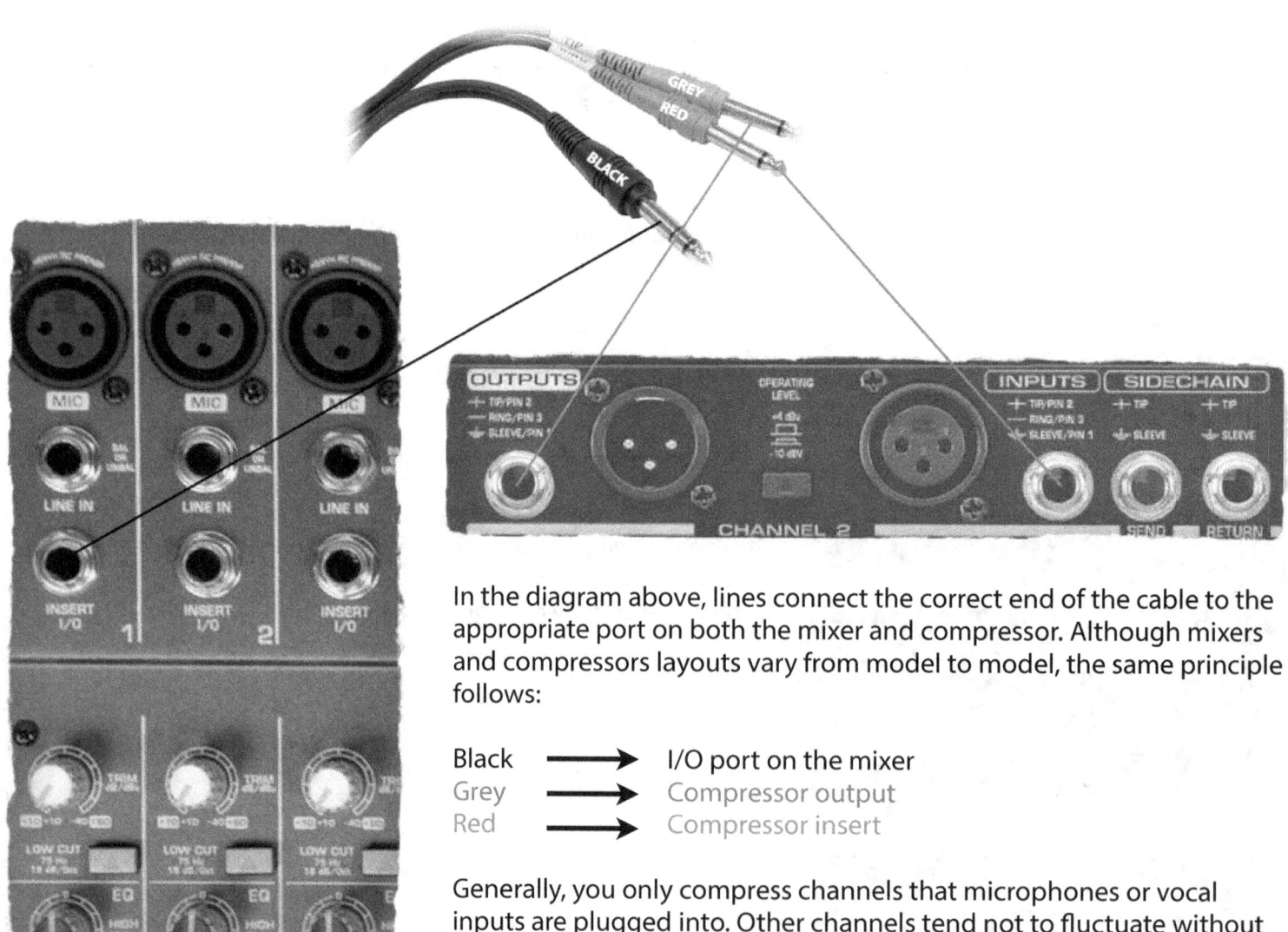

In the diagram above, lines connect the correct end of the cable to the appropriate port on both the mixer and compressor. Although mixers and compressors layouts vary from model to model, the same principle follows:

Black ⟶ I/O port on the mixer
Grey ⟶ Compressor output
Red ⟶ Compressor insert

Generally, you only compress channels that microphones or vocal inputs are plugged into. Other channels tend not to fluctuate without manual intervention or changes.

Compressors

Compressor Terms

Now you know how to setup a compressor, lets take a look at the terms and labels that are displayed under the dials on the compressor which can seem complicated, but really aren't.

Threshold: This is the set level/volume that the audio signal will begin to be compressed. A lower threshold will result in more of the overall signal being compressed, while a higher threshold will result in less overall signal being compressed. Audio below the threshold will not be compressed, audio above it will be compressed at the set ratio.

Ratio: The ratio determines at what rate the audio above the threshold will be reduced. A ratio of 1:1 will do nothing, because per every 1dB over the threshold 1dB will be outputted. A ratio of 2:1 means for every 2dB over the threshold, 1dB of the 2 will be outputted.

Attack: This is also known as the "reaction time". It determines how quickly or slowly the compressor will apply the compression from the point the threshold is crossed. The attack time is usually in milliseconds, typical ranges go from 1 millisecond to 100 milliseconds.

Release: This is the time which the "compressed" sound will return back to normal gain after the threshold is crossed in the opposite direction. The release time, is usually given in milliseconds to seconds. Typical ranges are from 25 milliseconds to 4 or more seconds.

Many compressors also include a "noise gate" - also known as expander/gate. A noise gate is used to stop noise below a specified volume from getting through. If you set your noise gate to allow audio above -25dB in, anything below that will not get through, or will be "rejected". See the diagram below for further explanation.

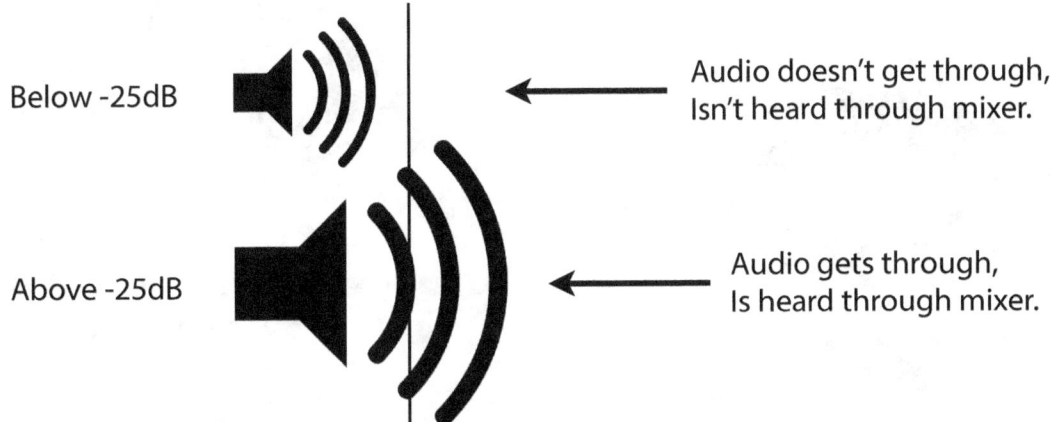

Cameras | 24

Chapter Summary

In this chapter, we'll take a look at the different types of camera's, and why good quality is important - as well as why you don't need to spend thousands to get a good quality camera.

Whether you are going to do video or not is a decision that you have to make - remember; if you are going to, it may add to the cost of equipment - but a good camera doesn't have to cost thousands!

Summary

If you are planning on having an audio and video podcast, it is important to make sure that both two elements are covered and are of good quality. You don't want to provide low quality, grainy footage to go alongside your podcast, even if your content is fantastic, it will degrade the overall quality of your show. Although, getting good video quality doesn't mean spending thousands!

Types of Camera's

There are hundreds, if not thousands of makes and models of cameras, which can make choosing the right one a difficult choice for some. There are a few options to choose from when it comes to cameras, which we'll take a look at.

Webcam - Although webcams may have a reputation for producing low quality, grainy footage (especially those built in computers and laptops) - there are high quality, HD webcams which don't cost a lot! These are probably the cheapest and most ideal option when choosing a camera. They allow easy connection (normally USB) and are compatible right out of the box. Two examples of HD webcams are the Microsoft LifeCam Studio which produces 1080p (full HD) video, and the Logitech C910 HD which produces 720p (HD) video. Both of these webcams are under $100!

Traditional Camera - Getting a good quality camera/camcorder can cost a lot of money! Especially if they output HD. Buying the camera is one thing, but if your computer doesn't have the correct input, you will have to buy additional hardware such as video and capture cards, which aren't always cheap! If you are, however wanting to go down this route a good choice is the Canon Vixia HF G10, which will require a converter to take the output to input it into your computer. If you're using a professional switcher which uses SDI, then an HDMI to SDI converter would be required (an example of which being the Blackmagic Design HDMI to SDI mini converter). However, if you're inputting into a PC you would require a Blackmagic intensity Pro. These capture card recommendations may not be suitable for your computer so check before purchasing anything!

Did you know?

Kodak engineer Steven Sasson developed the first digital camera prototype in 1975. It weighed 8lbs and had a resolution of only .01 megapixels!

Capture Cards

Chapter Summary

Capture cards are used to take the output of your camera/camcorder to input it in your computer in order for you to connect the camera.

Different camera's will require different capture cards, depending on what output your camera supports. Most modern camera's, along with the one we have recommended outputs HDMI.

Summary

A capture card will take the output signal from your camera and will allow you to input it into your computer. If the computer you're using to record and/or broadcast live has PCI (PCI, PCI Express) then you can use a capture card to plug your camera in directly to your computer.

What's Right For Me?

As noted before, different camera's will require different capture cards, depending on what output your camera supports. However, we'll assume in this chapter that your camera supports HDMI, as does the one we recommended on the previous page, the Canon Vixia HF G10.

How it Works

Once you have a capture card, you will have to connect it to your computer, remember, not all computers do support generic capture cards. If your computer has PCI or PCI Express then yours does. If it doesn't, you will have to look at purchasing a USB model. There are other connections but these two are the most common.

Once you have installed your capture card, connect your camera and make sure any additional necessary software is installed. The camera should now show up as an input.

A recommended capture card is the Blackmagic Intensity Pro.

Breakout Cable
(Analog video and audio connections)

HDMI Output
(HDTVs and video projectors)

HDMI Input
(HDMI input for cameras etc)

Did you know?

HDMI stands for High-Definition Multimedia Interface. It can carry uncompressed video and up to 8 audio channels.

Cables

Chapter Summary

Cables are essential for connecting audio and video equipment up. However, there are many types, some you may already be familiar with - and some you may not be.

We'll take a look at the most common and some that are going to of use when setting your equipment up.

Summary

Cables are used for connecting audio and video equipment. There are different types, which serve different purposes. We'll take a look at the most common, along with their uses.

Types of Cables

3.5mm - You're probably already familiar with this cable, as it is used in many headphones and earphones to connect them to MP3 players, phones etc.

1/4" - These are normally used by mixers and other equipment that connects to the mixer.

XLR - The XLR cable is used mostly for microphones, although other pieces of equipment do utilise it. The cable connects from your XLR microphone to your mixer input.

RCA - Otherwise known as the home stereo cable. It is a common cable for various audio equipment.

Insert Cable - The insert cable is used for connecting devices like compressors, EQ units etc. For information on using it, see back to the compressor section of this chapter which covers the cable in more depth, what it is used for and how to connect it.

Did you know?

Although most cables can be purchased cheaply, some audiophiles will pay tens of thousands for a high quality cables!

Show Preparation 27

Chapter Summary

In this chapter we will be taking a look at show preparation. This includes writing notes, doing research, guests and timings of your show.

This chapter will cover some of the best ways of preparing for each episode, helpful tips and useful sites that can all help with on of the most important tasks, preparing.

Summary

Preparing for your show is one of the most vital parts but is very often missed out by new podcasters. Many new podcasters plan the bare basics and try to go straight to recording, this can often leave unprepared parts of the shows with lots of silence and makes for awkward listening.

Methods of Preparing for Your Show

There are many different ways of preparing for your show, whether it is your 1st or your 100th episode, preparing is still a very valuable thing.

If you have a more casual show (non scripted) then you will need to prepare notes for your show. What is meant by notes? If you are doing a show that is all about the latest in technology of the week, then you will need notes of what you are going to talk about. Over the week you can accumulate links to articles that you think may be interesting to talk about. One tip to keep in mind is only select articles that you can talk about and that you have opinions on, not just to "bulk" up your show with stories that aren't relevant.

Make sure that you understand the article as well, you cannot relay information to your audience that is either wrong or that you don't understand. You will want to do some research about what you are talking about, take the time to look up and fully read about it, and even double check it from other news sources.

When gathering notes you will also need to take into account then length of your show, if your show is a news show and around an hour or so long then 6 or 7 show notes is sufficient. However, you may want some extra content incase you run through the earlier notes quickly.

If your show is going to be scripted, then you will need to write a script, make sure the script is lengthy enough to keep it going for the allocated time of your show.

For most types of podcasts an unscripted layout is the best idea, scripts are normally used if you are running a high production show. Some people find easier to read of an exact script. When doing this, the trick is to read from the script and sound natural whilst doing so.

Did you know?

More than 2 billion pens are manufactured in the United States alone annually.

Show Preparation

If you are not running a show where you can use articles and links then you can outline your show. Writing an outline for your show gives you an idea in which order you want to talk about things, it helps you stay on track in the middle of recording.

Here is a simple example of a show outline.

[Show name] Episode 1
1. **Intro music**
2. **Introduce [Show name]**
    1. What is the show about?
    2. What will it offer?
3. **Introduce yourself/host panel**
    1. What do you do for a living?
    2. What is your background?
    3. How did you get into podcasting?
    4. What are your hobbies?
4. **What should you expect from this show?**
    A) How often will this show be?
    B) What can you expect the show to be about each episode?
5. **Main portion of the show**
6. **Cue outro music**
7. **Talk over music giving out social links, information and thanks to your listeners or guests**
8. **End recording**

If you want you could colour code different parts of your outline if that makes different parts easier to understand. The outline is not designed to be the set in stone way of the show but more of a way to keep you on track during your show, if you forget what you wanted to talk about next then using an outline can really help get back on track.

You don't need to fill the outline with every little thing you want to say, just the main headings. You will soon get a system going and one that runs smoothly the more you do it, don't expect it to be perfect the first, second or even third time round, every episode you will always try and perfect something, tweak something or add something new.

Notes with pen and paper
Some people prefer to skip writing outlines, collecting links etc all together and just write their notes using pen and paper. Having a notebook handy with you throughout the week means that if you think of anything you want to talk about on the show then you can quickly note it down. With more and more people having smartphones these days there are also a number of applications that you can use to do the same thing, some of which are covered on the next page.

Show Preparation

Note Taking Services

Evernote
Everyone should be using Evernote, whether your podcasting or not. Evernote is a great service for taking tokes, you can easily save URLs and create text, image, audio or video notes.

From pretty much any application you can save things to Evernote by emailing them to your Evernote account. It's great for keeping notes for your show and can be useful for keeping your outline in. You can access Evernote from anywhere on almost any device.

Evernote offer a free service and they also offer a paid for service that gives you more storage.

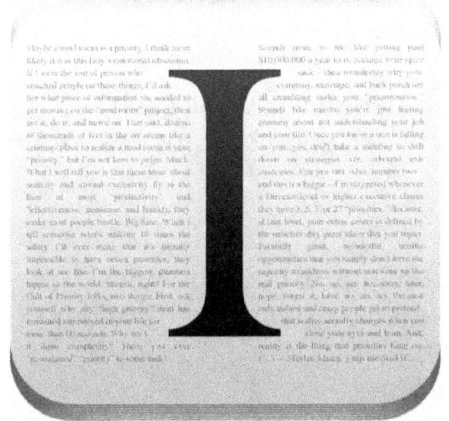

Instapaper
If you need an easy way to save articles then Instapaper is great. It allows you to easily save articles and then organise them into folders, you can create a folder for each show and then add the articles for that show or episode.

Many applications now offer integration with Instapaper allowing you to save directly to it.

Instapaper is free, but you can also subscribe for $1 a month and that gets you additional features, Quoted from Instapaper, "$3 for 3 months is less than a cup of coffee in most places."

Teleprompter

If you are using a script on your show and you are recording video then you may want to look into purchasing a teleprompter. A teleprompter is a mirrored screen system that displays the script in front of the camera, you look directly at the camera so people don't realise you are actually looking at a script.

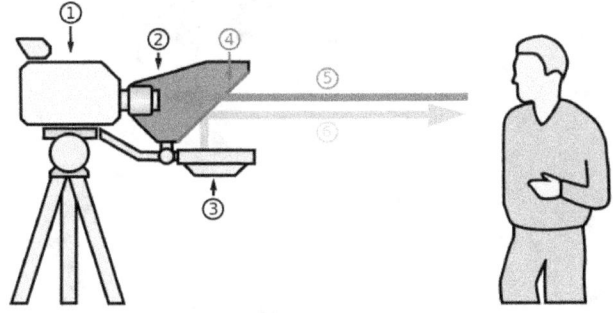

1. Video camera
2. Shroud
3. Video monitor
4. One-way mirror
5. Image from subject
6. Image from video monitor

Show Preparation

Guests

Having guests on your show can spice up the show for the listeners, it can also bring a new view on the things you are talking about. One of the obvious things to keep in mind when asking guest on your show is to make sure they are appropriate for the type of show, you do not want the guest to feel awkward because they don't know what you are talking about.

When emailing your guest put a variety of dates and times that suit you but remember that the times may not suit them so you will need to mention that if the times do not suit then they should suggest some new ones and you can work something out. Remember when setting times to record to check with them the timezone they are in, you can use a service like "worldtimebuddy.com" to check their timezone against yours. If you are using Skype for the interview then don't forget to give them your Skype name.

When it comes to recording time you'll want to make sure that you have everything prepared beforehand, you don't want to be wasting their time. Have all your questions and other stories/topics you want to talk about ready, you can create an outline like the one we talked about in the notes section in this chapter, with questions you want to ask.

You may be nervous the first time but the more and more you do it, the less nervous you will be. It's like meeting someone new in real life, you quickly get to know them and conversation becomes easier.

Timing Your Show

Unlike mainstream media, you do not have to be military precise with the timings of your show. It's your show and you're in control so you can start when you want and end when you want. In the outline we created earlier you can add time frames next to each part of the show, for example introducing the panel can be allotted around 5 mins. It should just be a rough idea and not exact. After the first few shows you should get an idea for how long each show should be and try and stick to that throughout.

If you find that your show is an hour long each time try and stick to that, listeners or viewers may be a little disappointed if your show is 1 hour one week, 20 mins the next and then 35 the next. Consistency is good.

Recording   31

Chapter Summary

In this chapter we will be taking a look at recording your show. Everything from recording video and audio to recording in the correct environment.

We'll look at some good software and hardware to help you record your show and some good tips for recording in a good environment and reducing noise in your show.

Summary

You've finished preparing, you've got all of your equipment set up and it's time to record a show, but where to start? There are a few different ways of recording your show. It's important to pick the right one that suits you and your show.

Before You Record

Before you record you need to make sure that the environment you are recording in is distraction free, you don't want loud noises or people walking in and out distracting you in the background. If your equipment set up is simple and you are only using a laptop (or a digital recorder) and a USB microphone then you have a wide variety of places you can choose to record. If your set up is a little more complicated and includes a desktop computer then you are limited to where you can go to record, the chances are that it is already in a good place as it is a desktop setup.

Some microphones are very sensitive to quiet noises even if they are outside the room so you'll want to find the perfect balance with the volume of the microphone so that people can still hear you clearly but the background noises are kept to minimum.

If your microphone is on a desk then you will want to avoid creating loud noises on the desk because they will go straight through to the microphone. Typing and even putting your hands or arms on the desk can create loud noises in the recording if the microphone is on your desk. You can reduce the noise by suspending your microphone off of the desk using something such as an mic stand.

You can reduce noise further by adding a shock mount. A microphone shock mount suspends the microphone by elastic so that there is nothing for vibrations to travel along. Normally the vibrations will travel along the metal and into the microphone but if you reduce the solid surfaces by suspending it in elastic, it will eliminate the noise from the microphone.

You may also invest in an on air light to let people know when you are recording so that the do not disturb you whilst you are in the middle of recording. Most podcasters won't need one but for some it may be useful if you want to avoid interruptions during recordings.

Did you know?

If you could stretch out into a straight line all of the data stored on a single CD, it would stretch for over 4 miles in total length.

Recording

Portable Sound Booth
If you want to reduce background noise and audio interference further then you can invest in a portable sound booth.

A portable sound booth allows you to get the professional studio sound at home without spending lots of money. Normally these are used for recording song lyrics but they are also great for podcasters as well. Most come with desk mounts illuminating the need to clamp it to a microphone stand and instead, right to your desk.

You'll find an entire list of our other microphone accessories recommendations in the equipment chapter of this book.

Digital Voice Recorders

If you are often on the move or are covering an event for your podcast then you may want to look into a digital voice recorder. Most have built in microphones of good quality and some offer audio input so you can record using your own microphone. Most have built in storage, and some also offer expandable storage via an SD (or micro SD) card that allows you to record more that the built in storage will allow.

Some MP3 players offer the ability to record audio but they will not normally record above CD quality. Portable audio recorders will record high quality, professional grade audio which is why they are useful for a variety of scenarios, in this case recording your podcast.

Some people use a digital recorder as a backup recorder, if their computer crashes midway through the show and it has lost the recording then you have a backup file on the audio recorder.

If you are walking around recording your podcast, traveling and want to record, or you're covering an event for your podcast then investing in one of these can really save having to carry around a big laptop and complicated setup. Most of these recorders are light weight and compact.

Recording 33

Zoom H1

Zoom are known for making some great audio products and they make some great portable digital audio recorders.

The Zoom H1 is an affordable audio recorder that is feature packed and suitable for most use cases. It has an X/Y microphone pattern that is said to record "stereo sound with remarkable depth and clarity".

You can add up to a 32 GB microSDHC card for storage. Audio unlike video will take up a lot less room, so 32 GB can record up 50 hours of audio in 16-bit/44.1 kHz WAV or up to 555 hours in 128 kbps MP3 format.

It includes a built-in low cut filter that reduces unwanted background noise by cutting out anything below a certain frequency.

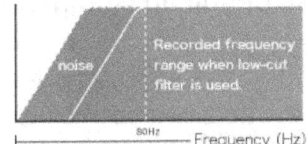

One of the best features about the H1 is the ability to add external microphones and line level sources. The H1's stereo microphone input jack (3.5mm) can provide plug-in power, allowing you to utilise additional microphones as needed. The jack also accepts stereo line-level inputs such as cassette decks, record players and other analog sources.

Zoom offer a hot shoe mount so that you can attach it to a camera and use the H1 to record high quality audio to go along with your video, this is great for video podcasters who want a super simple home set up or the ability to record great audio on the move.

The Zoom H1 will set you back anywhere around £70 - £100 depending on where you buy from. This may seem a lot but if you compare that price to some of the others in the market it's actually fairly affordable.

Zoom H4

The Zoom H4 is far from cheap but has amazing quality and some great features that you may or may not find useful. Unlike most low end recorders, it has a 1/4" input as well as an XLR input! Perfect for connecting your mixer, or even just a microphone up for recording out of your home studio, if required. It also has two separate microphones at the top which produce good quality audio for interviewing someone at an event, or yet again, outside your home studio. It doesn't come cheap, however - costing upwards of £250! It's not completely justifiable if you want a cheap backup to your software recording, so you might want to consider one of the cheaper ones. Like most digital recorders, the Zoom H4 uses an SD card to store the recordings which can be taken out and connected to a computer.

Recording

Edirol R-05

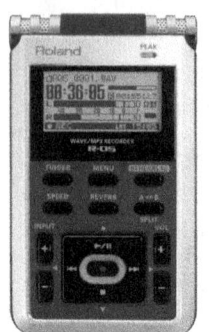

The Edirol R-05 is slightly cheaper, but is yet again one of the higher end digital recorders. It doesn't have the advanced input of the Zoom H4 and accepts the standard 3.5mm jack. It also gives you the ability to record in .mp3 and .wav format for higher quality, if required. It too records onto an SD card for easy transfer from the device to a computer. You can also connect the device to your computer by way of USB to allow you to transfer recordings without removing the SD card. It runs around the £200 mark, and again, if you're looking for a cheap recording backup, isn't really necessary.

Sony ICD-UX512

The Sony ICD-UX512 is a cheaper, but nearly as versatile as higher end recorders. It has the standard 3.5mm jack to connect your mixer up to, as well as 2GB of built in storage, and a card slot for additional storage!

It runs around the £50 mark and is a lot more justifiable than buying a higher end recorder; especially if you're just wanting to use it to backup your recordings incase of loosing your recording through a power cut, or your computer crashing.

Audio Software

For most beginners using software to record your show is the obvious option. Choosing the right software is important, you wouldn't want the app to crash mid recording due to it being an unstable app.

Audacity

Audacity is one of the most famous and widely used pieces of audio software out there, why? Because it's free. Audacity is available for Mac, Windows and Linux and it is a very simple app to use and it offers a large array of features and functions.

Audacity is said to record and edit in 16-bit, 24-bit and 32-bit (floating point) samples and can record up to 96 kHz sample rate. Audacity allows you to add effects such as a compressor that can even out the peaks in your audio, the effects are average and are not great but are more than enough for most beginners. One thing to mention is that when you apply an effect you are permanently changing that audio file so make sure you keep an original copy of the audio file. You cannot go back when you apply an effect or tweak the EQ again.

While Audacity may not be for music production or people looking for something professional, it is a great audio editor for adding simple effects and your podcast intro and ending music and not to mention, it's free.

Recording

Adobe Audition

Audition is a professional piece of kit and it's price tag shows it. It's not cheap at £333 (boxed retail) but it is well worth the money if you are looking to step your audio production up a gear.

Some audio professionals still overlook Adobe Audition due to its lack of support for control surfaces along with other features, but for most pro podcasters and for general audio production Audition is top notch software. The effects are really well thought out and a well equipped for most your needs, each effect can be tweaked further to just the right settings for you. If you do not have a hardware compressor for example for you can add a compressor effect to your audio track or to a specific part of your audio track. Both Audacity and Audition allow multi-track recording as that is a very basic audio editing feature.

If you are looking for a professional piece of software and want to spend a little extra to get better audio then Adobe Audition is well worth the price tag. Audition is available on both the Mac and the PC.

GarageBand

GarageBand is only useful if you have a Mac as it is part of the iLife suite. GarageBand is by no means a competitor to the likes of Adobe Audition. It is more of a competitor to Audacity than anything, you will not be producing the chart topper with this but you may well be able to produce a decent sounding podcast.

GarageBand comes with a whole heap of audio loops that you can use as your intro music or even background music throughout. As a tip, using these loops may sound cliché as they have been used many a time before by other podcasters.

WireTap Studio

This one is again for Mac users. WireTap is a super simple audio recorder that allows you to record either one or two of your Macs audio inputs. You can also record different software on your Mac, WireTap is a good solution for recording you and your guests through Skype if you're using a USB microphone and don't use a mixer. WireTap offers very simple audio editing and the ability to export your audio in a variety of formats. Unlike Audacity, WireTap allows "non destructive" audio effects and you can apply a wide variety of effects whilst you record. WireTap is a useful and simple but yet feature packed piece of software. The Studio version is around £44 ($69) but is well worth the money for the app it is.

Recording   36

Video Software

If you are creating a video podcast and you are not using the record function on the camera then you need to pick the right software. Video recording software can be more resource intense so you will need a fairly powerful computer to run them. We have covered a lot of video software in the 'Broadcasting Live' chapter but we will recap it here.

Wirecast

Wirecast allows you to easily take multiple video inputs and record to disk and/or broadcast it live. You can overlay graphics onto your video easily. Wirecast is a video production tool that mixes multiple inputs, adds transitions, titles and other different effects. One of the biggest features of Wirecast for people doing video production in front of a green screen is that you can do chroma keying to add backgrounds to your video. For example, if you wanted to make it look like you were in a news room set. With chroma keying and a green screen you can, with Wirecast. It is most commonly used by podcasters as it is competitively priced compared with other video production software on the market. It still doesn't come cheap at $449 for the standard version. Despite this price tag, just by the sheer number of podcasters using it, you can say that Wirecast is probably one of the best live video production applications out, in it's price range.

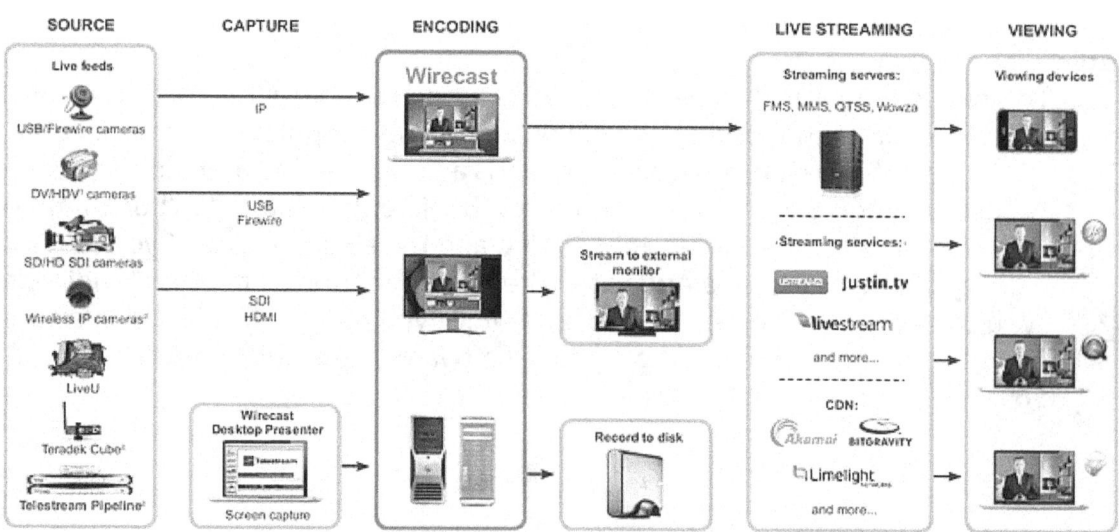

Recording   37

BoinxTV

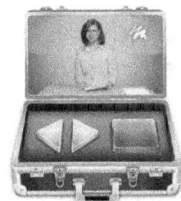

BoinxTV is very similar to Wirecast apart from one of the bigger downsides that it does not allow you to broadcast live, you can record directly to your hard disk and you can see a preview but there is no way of broadcasting live directly from this app.

Like Wirecast, BoinxTV offers the ability to overlay text and graphics and also the ability to chroma key. When creating a video podcast you do not want to be sitting around waiting for things to work, you want to be able to record high quality video quickly and efficiently. Both of these applications reduce the need to edit the video after (live to disk) which saves a lot of time, as editing, rendering and exporting video can take up to hours on end meaning if you do choose to do it that way you may want to grab a coffee, or two.

The new updates to BoinxTV have added better audience integration allowing you to display Twitter streams via video and also take in viewer's Skype calls. Both BoinxTV and Wirecast are great for video production and more importantly podcasters. BoinxTV is a resource hog, it bogs the computer down so that it is almost unusable. So, if possible - you may want to run it on a separate machine unless your computer is powerful.

VidBlaster

VidBlaster is the be all, end all video production software and it comes with a price tag to show that. If you are looking to really step video production up a notch then VidBlaster is the product to use. Wirecast and BoinxTV are already professional pieces of kit so for most there is no need to upgrade to the higher tiers of VidBlaster. However, if you are looking for something that does most (if not all) of the things you need, then VidBlaster Home may be for you. If you are looking to create a full blown broadcast environment then you may want to take a look at some of the higher tiered versions.

When setting up your video recording software you will want to make sure that it is recording in the highest quality that your video inputs will produce. If your cameras produce a resolution of 1280X720 (pixels 720P/I) then you will want to make sure that your recording software is set to record in that or higher. For both audio and video you will want to do a test recording right before you record the actual show so that you can make sure that all of the audio and video levels are OK.

Recording 38

Recording Guests or Co-Hosts over Skype

Now you know the various utilities and applications for recording audio and video, lets take a look at recording guests or co-hosts over Skype. There are various methods for doing this, some easier than others. We'll take a look at both.

Using a Mixer (Mix Minus)

If you have decided to use a mixer, you can use it to your advantage. In order to record a Skype call using mix minus, you'll need a mixer that has "auxiliary (aux) outputs". Mix Minus is sometimes difficult to understand, but once you do understand the concept it's very easy to setup.

The theory of mix minus is that the audio your guest or co-host hears (over Skype, or other VOIP applications) includes all audio **but** their voice. In other words, they hear everything that is being recorded, but themselves. This means feedback and echo is avoided and the person on the other end cannot hear themselves.

Setting up Mix Minus is easy, it is only easily possible to achieve if your mixer has one (or more) auxiliary output(s).

Let's assume that your Skype computer **output** is connected to input 3 on your mixer. The input to your Skype computer from your mixer is fed through an aux channel, for example, Aux 1. Turn the Aux 1 dial to 12 o'clock on all of the channels you want to send to the Skype computer, but make sure **not** to turn the dial of the Skype **input**, otherwise, the person on the other end will be able to hear themselves back. The idea is that you are creating a MIX for the Skype computer that is MINUS the Skype audio. Most podcasters will set and leave every channel (except the Skype channel) so that the caller can hear everything going on.

Recording Skype Without a Mixer

If you have decided to use a USB microphone, or headset, you can still record Skype calls. However, you'll need separate software or applications to do so. There are quite a few Skype call recorders on the market. Both applications listed below are extremely simple to use and are very self explanatory to use. They simply allow you to record your audio and the person on Skype's audio, and mixes them together into one recording.

 Pamela for Skype ($33) Windows only

Call Recorder for Skype ($20) Mac only.

 You can also use **WireTap** to record your entire show, and your guest at the same time. Mac only. (**$69**)

Broadcasting Live

Chapter Summary

In this chapter we'll look at different live broadcasting services and reasons for and against broadcasting your show live.

Broadcasting your show live has many advantages and a few disadvantages. It can be as complex or as simple as you want.

Summary

Many podcasters choose to broadcast their shows live as they record, but some also choose not to. There are many great services out there for broadcasting your show live and most are even free. There are also different types of live broadcasting, for example are you going to be doing live video and audio or just live audio? The type of broadcast you do effects the cost of doing the show live.

Why Broadcast Live?

Broadcasting your show live as you record may help you gain more listeners or viewers. The discovery functions on many live streaming sites allow the users to find new content that may be specific to them, i.e. if someone was watching a tech show live on Ustream, in the related section other tech shows are displayed. Your show may pop up in that related section if it is a tech show. Getting discovered by people is always the hardest part of having a podcast, so broadcasting your show can really boost the discovery of your show.

Video or Audio?

Some podcasters chose to do live video and audio broadcasts whilst some choose only to do live audio. Video comes with its costs as you need a lot of video equipment, whereas with audio you can just take the input that you are recording and broadcast it.

If your podcast is already doing video then live video should not be as costly as you already have most of the equipment needed. If your podcast is currently audio only then a similar situation applies, you already have most of the needed equipment to start a live show easily. The decision to do either type of live show is mostly based on what equipment you have, if you are willing to go out and spend a little more money and get the right equipment for doing live video then that is a good option. If you are not as willing then audio may be the way for now, remember you can always change at any point.

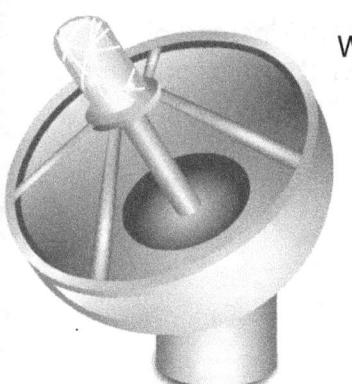

We'll take a look later in this chapter at equipment for both audio and video. We will also be taking a look at different software that can accompany the equipment as well as software replacements for hardware.

Did you know?

On November 4, 1994, Stef van der Ziel distributed the first live video images over the web from the Simplon venue in Groningen.

Broadcasting Live

Cameras

A pretty obvious piece of equipment, but one that needs to be taken seriously. We have covered cameras heavily in the equipment chapter of this book. See that chapter for camera recommendations.

Good quality cameras are always a bonus but if you are not streaming in HD and you do not plan on streaming in HD, then you do not need to spend a lot on HD cameras. If you plan on streaming HD in the future or want to do HD straight away then will need to purchase HD camera(s). Remember that streaming in high definition requires a lot more bandwidth than standard definition so you'll want to make sure you have an Internet connection that can handle it. Anywhere between 2-3Mbps upload speed should be fine for HD, you can check your speed by using a speed checker online such as "speedtest.net."

Video Switcher

The video switcher is probably one of the more expensive pieces of equipment so we will look more in the software part of this chapter about how you can do practically the same without the huge price tag using software alone. A video switcher allows you change between different video inputs live. For example if you have 2 cameras you can use a switcher to easily change between the 2 cameras.

If you are looking for the best results then a Newtek Tricaster is the best but it does not come cheap by any stretch. You'll find that many TV stations and live broadcasters will use a Tricaster or something very similar, this is because they constantly have to switch between many different cameras and inputs.

Newtek offers a variety of different switchers and control surfaces. They allow you to add graphics to your video such as lower thirds to display people's names at the bottom of the screen (in the lower third).

A cheaper video switcher that only works with software is using the Korg Nanokontrol. This is not actually a video switcher but a tweak using some software can make it into one with Wirecast on the Mac. If you do a Google search for "Korg Nanokontrol Wirecast", that will lead you to it.

It is not that difficult to setup and is great it you want a video switcher for around £30/$50 instead of getting a Tricaster for thousands. Remember that the Tricaster (or any other similar switcher) will out perform a software switcher as it is dedicated hardware, and has been specifically designed with all needs in mind.

Broadcasting Live   41

Video Capture Cards

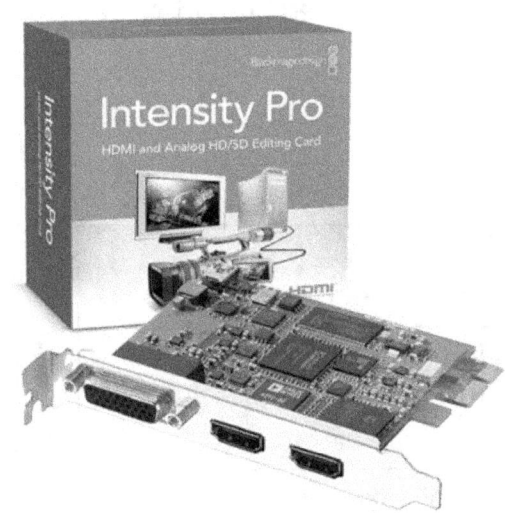

If the computer you are using to broadcast live has PCI (PCI, PCI Express) then you can add a video capture card that adds video inputs to the computer. You can plug your camera(s) directly into the capture card and the computer should recognize it as another video input. This is like plugging your USB webcam in but for more professional cameras that have either HDMI, mini HDMI, composite or any other type of video output.

A capture card can be a cheaper alternative to hardware switchers but will require software to make use of the video inputs.

Capture cards often support either standard definition and high definition or sometimes even both.

USB video capture cards are also available and they are cheaper than PCI ones but this comes at an expense. The PCI cards will out perform the USB ones as the connection bandwidth is greater so the speed in which video is transferred is better. This allows for a much smoother video input. If you are not looking to pay more money for a PCI card then a USB card should do the job fine.

One of the most famous video capture cards is the intensity Pro from Blackmagic. Blackmagic are known widely in the industry for their video hardware. The Intensity Pro card is an affordable video card that combines HDMI capture and playback with analog component, PAL and S-video. Live streaming with this card means that you get uncompressed video source. Meaning the CPU does not waste any resources tying to decompress the video whilst capturing.

When purchasing USB capture cards online, be cautious. There are many fake models resembling real models which either do a horrible job or don't work at all!

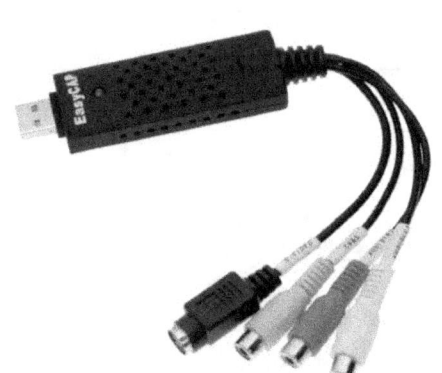

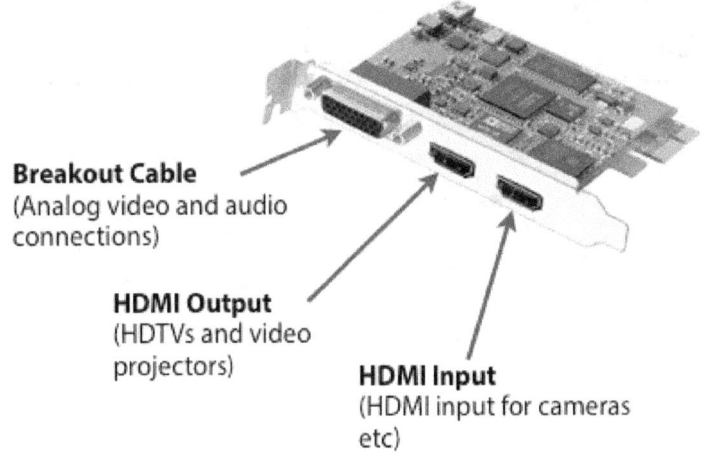

Breakout Cable
(Analog video and audio connections)

HDMI Output
(HDTVs and video projectors)

HDMI Input
(HDMI input for cameras etc)

Broadcasting Live

Software

Some hardware may need to be combined with software or can even be replaced by software for a lower cost. In this section we'll be taking a look at some of the software that can be used both in conjunction with hardware and some that is it's own standalone software.

Software	Cost	OS	Broadcast From App	Pros and Cons
Wirecast	$449 Pro $995	Mac/Windows	✓	• Best option for live streaming • Easy to understand • Powerful
Boinx TV	$449	Mac	✗	• Many Possibilities • Resource Hog • No live streaming support built in
Ustream Producer	Free Pro $199 Studio $549	Mac/Windows	✓	• Free version available (limited) • Resembles Wirecast • Can only stream to Ustream
Vidblaster	Home $232 Pro $589 Studio $1184 Broadcast $2374	Windows	✓	• Very professional and powerful • Different versions suit different needs • Professional effects and tools
Flash Media Live Encoder	Free	Mac/Windows	✓	• Difficult to setup compared to others • Streams audio and video in real time • Delivers good results • Free • Widely supported

Broadcasting Live

What is Video Encoding?

We have mentioned several times in previous pages about media encoders but what exactly is video encoding?

All of the videos we watch on our computers, tablets, phones, TV's, etc. all have to be converted into the suitable format for that device. Video encoding is the process of converting digital video files from one format to another.

When encoding video you must consider:

- The original source and capture methods
- Encodes that will be performed later
- The intended output of the video, i.e. Where is it going? YouTube? TV?

Streaming Audio

If you want to stream audio alone for something like an Internet radio station then you can use an application called Icecast. This gives you the ability to take a sound output and stream it to a server or over a network as an Internet radio stream. You have to install some software on the server so for help doing that you may need to contact your hosting provider and they should be able to help you out. Some services also sell dedicated hosting boxes solely for streaming audio only.

Shoutcast radio is an alternative to this, it is far simper to get up and running as there is an extensive range of support out there as it is an ongoing project.

Shoutcast servers and clients are available for a wide variety of platforms such as FreeBSD, Linux, Mac OSX, Windows and Solaris. There are also client-only versions on Android, Blackberry OS, iOS, Palm OS and Web OS, Playstation Portable, Windows Mobile and a few others.

Editing

Chapter Summary

Editing is the process of "cleaning up" your recording. Whether that is removing silences, adding sound effects or changing the overall sound - it is all done in editing.

There are multiple methods, and multiple applications that can help make the editing process much easier.

Summary

There are multiple methods of editing, all of which have their advantages and disadvantages. We'll take a look at these and look at editing applications.

Two Options

The first thing to consider is whether you want to edit in what is known as "post production" - this basically consists of adding intro and outro music, sound effects and other edits after recording. Or if you're going to edit "live to disk", otherwise known as "live editing". Both of which have their advantages and disadvantages which we'll look at.

Post Production

Post production consists of recording just the vocal side of your podcast and then editing your music and other sound effects in after the fact. This takes a lot longer to do and can sometimes get tedious trying to find a certain part of your show to add an effect, jingle or clip. This time could of course be used for preparing your next episode. However, it does allow for more intricate editing, allowing you to make small adjustments to your recording.

Live to Disk

Live to Disk (live editing) speeds the process up a lot! It consists of hitting the record button and playing your jingle music live, while you control the music and other tracks with your mixer. This option allows you to monitor your music as it's being played and if there is something that needs changing then you can do it live, instead of having to do it after recording! In order to play your jingles live, an application known as a "sound cart", or "soundboard" comes in handy. One recommendation is "SoundByte" by Black Cat Systems. This allows you to organise audio files into a table type of view, making it much easier to play multiple pieces at once.

A mixer definitely comes in useful when it comes to Live to Disk editing - in fact, without a mixer it is virtually impossible, unless you use a software equivalent. In one channel on the mixer, you will have your microphone, in another possibly a guest, then your cart application etc. This allows you to mix these inputs into one output - which is your live edited audio recording. The advantage of live editing is that it is far more efficient, meaning you're spending less time editing and more time preparing - which will, in the end make your show's production values better! Even with live editing, you'll still use editing software to export your recording. Exporting is the process of compressing your recording into a file that you can upload as your podcast.

Editing   45

Editing Applications
Whether you decide to edit in post production, or live to disk - you'll still need to utilise editing applications. We'll take a look at a few options, some of which are free and some of which cost.

Audacity
Audacity is free, open-source software which is compatible with Mac, Windows and Linux. It has some powerful editing tools which will help you cut and edit your show together. There are also effects and filters which may come in useful for your show.

Adobe Audition

Adobe Audition is a paid for application, which is used by industry professionals. The decision to buy it shouldn't be taken lightly - the need for it to beginner podcasters especially, isn't very high. It does allow more in depth editing and more features, however, these aren't completely necessary to record and edit your podcast professionally.

While it is a great application, it is far from free and again, really isn't needed to create an excellent podcast. Especially if you're just starting off.

GarageBand
If you're a Mac user and you've purchased iLife, you already have an application which will allow you to record and edit your new podcast! GarageBand, similar to other applications allows you to record and edit your show all in the one application. It also includes jingles that you can use on your show to spice it up and give it that professional sound! GarageBand isn't free, however it does come in the suite "iLife" for your Mac which also includes iMovie, iPhoto and other applications which you may find useful.

Exporting Your Show
Once you've edited your podcast, you need to export it. Exporting is the process of compressing your recording into a file that you can upload as your podcast. When exporting, there are many settings to choose from, which can seem intimidating - but they aren't! Far from it, actually. A common misconception is that the higher the number on the setting, the better quality. While theoretically this is correct (especially for music), for vocal podcasts - high quality export settings just aren't needed!

Editing

Recommended Export Settings:

Voice podcasts don't need to be exported in high quality settings - as it is just voice. Of course, if you were exporting music, this would be a different situation. The goal is to have a great sounding audio file, while keeping the size of the exported file as small as possible.

You'll want to export to ".mp3" - this is the format of the file. MP3 is not only the most compatible and flexible format, but it keeps the size of your file manageable. Nearly every device is compatible with MP3 allowing as many people to listen to your show as possible.

You'll want to set your "sample type" to 44,100Hz, this is perfect for audio, voice podcasts. Under the "channels" option make sure it is set to "mono" and not "stereo". You're probably thinking that stereo is better than mono, so why change it? With voice podcasts, you don't need stereo. Setting it to mono will make your end file smaller, with no real noticeable effect to your audio.

Summary of Export Settings:
Format - MP3
Sample Type - 44,100Hz, Mono
Format Settings - MP3, 64Kbps CBR (Constant Bitrate)

When naming your episode files, instead of naming them differently every episode; give them a generic filename, in other words; have the title of your show, then the episode number - e.g; "yourshowname001.mp3" - This means that it is easier for you (and your listeners) to access the files and you'll be able to go back to previous episodes easily.

ID3 Tagging

Once you've exported your podcast, you'll want to ID3 tag it. ID3 is a metadata "container" that allows information such as the title, artist as well as artwork to be stored in the file itself. There are various ways to ID3 tag a file, some of which we'll cover.

First off, what's the difference in an audio file with no ID3 tags and one with? On the next page are two images. One with a photo of an episode of one of our shows (The Two Techies) with ID3 tagging and one without.

Editing

Without ID3 Tagging   With ID3 Tagging

The photos were taken on an iPod, but the same basic rule applies on any other device or application, such as iTunes. If you don't ID3 tag your episodes you won't get any artwork on the actual file (as pictured on the photo above, on the left). If you do ID3 tag, you will (as pictured above, on the right).

A frequent question is "my artwork is showing on the iTunes Store, so why not on the episode" - that's exactly why, the episode files aren't being ID3 tagged! It's extremely simple to do. You can either use a piece of software dedicated to ID3 tagging, or of course, you can simply use iTunes by importing the file, right clicking and selecting "Get Info". Add the title, artist and description along with artwork, save and export the file - your file is now tagged!

Even though ID3 tagging is extremely simple, it is essential to make your end file more polished and professional - many people listen and consume podcasts on their portable devices, and seeing a default MP3 image will not be as glamorous as your show artwork.

Video Editing

Editing video can be time consuming, and more intensive on your computer which is a reason for considering audio only podcasts. But it is a decision you have to make yourself, there are advantages to doing video, as well as disadvantages. Many people who subscribe to podcasts listen to them when they are otherwise occupied, i.e. in the car, going to the gym, doing work etc. which means that they are unable to watch the video, and only the audio is consumed.

Editing

If video is something you feel would be beneficial to your podcast, by all means, go for it! In this section, we'll look at software you can use to edit your video podcast. Although live to disk editing is possible with video, exporting is still necessary which can be quite time consuming. Most video podcasts will go through post production of some sort.

Post Production

Post production is a lot more common when it comes to video - after all, the end file is a lot larger than the end file of audio. There is a wide range of software to choose for editing your podcast, some of which we'll look at.

Final Cut Pro X - Mac

Final Cut Pro is Apple's own application that industry professionals use to produce movies, television shows and the like. This doesn't mean however, that it can't be used by a podcaster. With older versions of Final Cut, this wouldn't have been a cheap option, with Final Cut costing upwards of £1000 ($1500+)! However, Apple noticed that many people were looking for a professional application for a fraction of the cost. Now, with the release of Final Cut Pro X, Final Cut may be slightly more viable with it costing £199 ($299).

iMovie - Mac

If FCP X is still slightly over budget, then there are cheaper alternatives, such as iMovie; which is included with Apple's iLife suite, which we looked at earlier when looking at GarageBand. iMovie offers many features, filters and options which will help you edit and export your video podcast in no time!

Sony Vegas - PC

For PC users, Sony Vegas is a near equivalent to Final Cut Pro, for Windows. Sony Vegas is a fully fledged video editing package which has the essentials for editing video, and more, perfect for editing podcasts on a PC.

Live to Disk

Live to Disk video editing isn't always easy - certainly not as easy as plain audio "live to disk" editing. Everything you want to add needs to be "cued" up, ready to go, to be played. Including your video and audio intro, outro and other elements you may want to add such as lower thirds.

Wirecast - Mac and PC

Wirecast follows the interface of that of a hardware switcher, instead it's contained within software. Starting at £310 ($499), the price may seem quite high, however; for the features included the price may be justifiable. It allows you to record, broadcast and export all from the app - allowing for live editing.

Editing

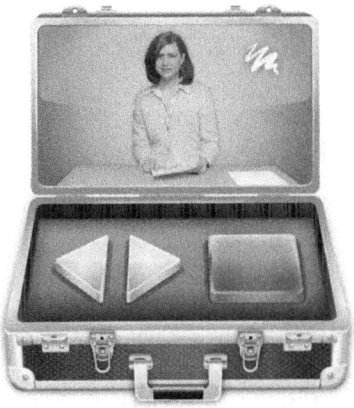

BoinxTV - Mac
BoinxTV also allows for live video editing and recording, however lacks a feature to broadcast your video live - there are ways of getting around this, such as using other software to capture part of the screen showing a preview of your "live" video, however this can become complex and annoying for you to control.

BoinxTV is available for £349 ($499), if this is too steep, however, a "lighter" version is offered, known as "BoinxTV Home" which will run you only £34 ($49).

VidBlaster - PC
VidBlaster has multiple versions, which offer different features, depending on what version you purchase. The cheapest option is "VidBlaster Home". The application allows you to edit your video podcast live, broadcast live and export as a video file to upload online.

The application you choose depends completely on what you want to be able to do, and what your budget is. Of course, that is if you want to do video alongside audio at all - remember, audio podcasts are sometimes the preferred format. There isn't a set rule, it's completely up to you, just remember that not everyone will be watching your video as they may be otherwise occupied with other tasks.

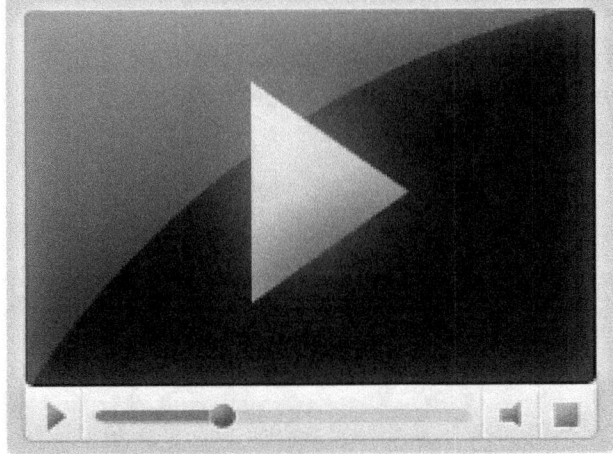

Remember, as a rule, video takes a lot more time, and computer power to edit, render and export than audio. Whether you are going to do video or not is a decision that has many factors to it. Some, which are for video being "it gives your audience a choice" and "it adds to the production values", and factors which are against such as "it takes a lot more time to produce" and "a lot of your audience will play your podcast when doing other tasks, meaning they're not actually watching the video, instead just listening to the audio."

Hosting

Chapter Summary

In this chapter we will be taking a look at hosting your podcast.

There are various services and methods for hosting your podcast. There are also some places where you shouldn't host your podcast. All of which, we'll cover in this chapter.

Summary

Hosting your podcast is an obvious step in the podcast creation process but choosing the right host can be difficult. There are hundreds of different ways you can host your episodes, all the way from using your own hosting to using a professional and dedicated podcast hosting service.

Why is it Important?

You may think that hosting your show is easy, you can just put it up on your web hosting that you are using for your website and be done with it. There are many reasons why you want to avoid doing that. One of the most common types of website hosting is shared hosting which by the title means that you are not the only one of that server. If you try and host large audio or video files they will be extremely slow to download for your listeners, and no one wants to wait hours for a podcast to download.

Some web hosts may even ban your account if you start hosting large files on their servers as most may have a fair usage policy that prohibits it. Audio will be easier to host on your web host as the file size is considerably smaller compared with video. When you have got your export settings right (see 'Editing' chapter) for audio then your file size should easily be under 50MB. Video can easily run into the gigabytes for a file, especially if you are recording and exporting in HD.

It is recommended that you look for a dedicated hosting service for your episodes. You can either look for a dedicated web hosting service that will allow you to host your large files (get in contact with them before you buy) or you can look into a podcast hosting service. There are dedicated hosting services for both audio and video podcasts and we'll take a look at some of the best in this chapter. If you are looking for web hosting then check out the 'Podcast Website' chapter for recommendations. A few things you will want to make sure that the hosting service you are choosing offers are statistics, a fair amount or even unlimited bandwidth and an ad free service. If you are paying for a service the last thing you want them to be doing is inserting ads in your files. Statistics are something very basic that every podcast hosting service should offer.

Check how much bandwidth they allow you to use, for example some web hosts allow unlimited bandwidth (fair usage policy applies) and that allows as many people to visit your site as possible. Every time someone visits your site that server has to transfer over data. This is called bandwidth. The same applies for podcast hosting services, every time an episode is delivered to someone bandwidth is required to serve it.

Did you know?

72 hours of video are uploaded to YouTube every minute and that number is increasing week on week!

Hosting

Blip.TV

Blip.TV are the Libsyn of the video world. They offer a huge range of features from hosting, distribution all the way to monetisation of your show. They also offer all of this for free, they do have a pro account which offers a lot of features the free plan doesn't which is expected. If you opt for the pro account then you get HD video quality support which for some is a must, if you upload HD content they will also automatically offer a SD version of it for devices that do not support HD playback. The pro account also offers the ability to automatically offer a transcoded MP3 edition of the video content if you want to offer an audio only version.

Blip.TV is the swiss army knife of the video world and even more so when you upgrade to the pro version. Blip.TV pro accounts cost $8 (£5) a month.

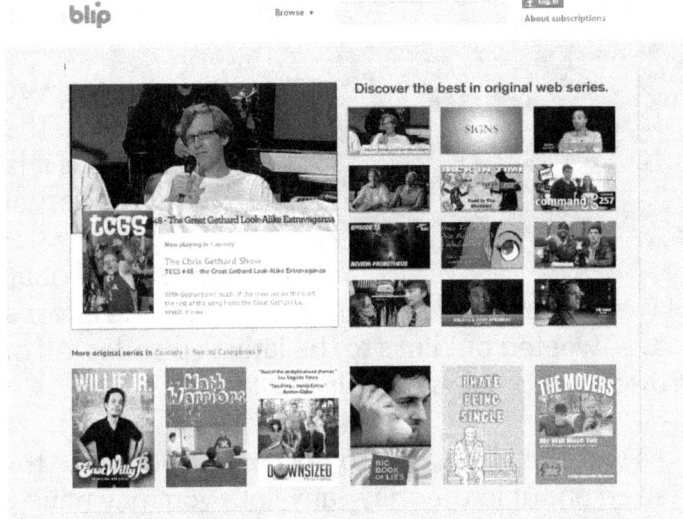

Blip.TV pride themselves on being 100% non-exclusive which means that they can distribute your show to a wide variety of services automatically such as iTunes, YouTube, Facebook, Twitter and more. They also offer analytics so you can track downloads and views of your episodes. Their player can be embedded on almost any website and you can offer ads in your content when you use their player. All of these features mentioned in the paragraph are available in the free account.

When choosing the service you will be using to host your podcast make sure that they include all of the features you want. Also make sure that you are not going to be paying for features and options that you don't need and only pay for the features and in some cases, space that you do need.

Podcast Website

> **Chapter Summary**
>
> In this chapter we will be taking a look at setting up and creating a website for your podcast.
>
> We'll cover how it can be beneficial to your podcast, and recommend some good plugins and themes for Wordpress, look at some services for creating the site and some services that can help speed up your site.

Summary

Having a website for your podcast is a must, without one you will be left behind. There are a wide range of services that you can use to make one and we'll look at those a bit later on. Before you even start creating though you need to think about where you will be hosting and what your domain will be.

Why?

As mentioned in the summary, having a website for your podcast is almost a must, without one you risk being left behind. A website is a great way for people to discover your show. They can also go back and listen to older episodes and find out more about your podcast. If you have multiple podcasts or shows then you can keep them all under one place on a website.

You can use your website as a extra revenue stream as you'll be able to place ads on it. There are endless reasons why it is important to have a website as it is hugely beneficial to your podcast in both in terms of usefulness and in terms of exposure.

If you take a look at any podcast you will more than likely find some sort of web page that is kept up to date with the latest episodes, it may even be a Twitter page where they have Tweeted out links to the latest episodes. All of that is online exposure for them that is aiding in the discovery process of their podcast.

Having a website allows you to post extra content to the site. Extra content can include the notes you have talked about in the show, any links you may have mentioned and other content you have talked about. You can link back to it from the show instead of trying to read the links out, this can also help push traffic to your website, more traffic can mean more money. If people want to find out more about a certain story or subject you talked about or mentioned you can link to it on your website so people can find out more themselves.

If you use a CMS (explained later) then you can do an individual post for each episode of the show. This then allows you to add the appropriate notes and links that are related to that episode. Keeping your content organised can deeply impact the usability of your site, keeping it organised now can also save you a headache down the road and makes searching trough the archives easier.

> **Did you know?**
>
> In many surveys, podcasters find that more than 60% of their listeners play the content straight from the creator's website rather than on a portable device.

Podcast Website

Choosing a Domain

Choosing a domain is an important step in setting up a website as it is what a user types in to navigate to your website. Nowadays it is becoming more and more difficult to find a good domain name that is available as most of the good ones have been taken, don't let that put you off though as one you like may well still be available.

There are a few things you need to keep in mind when choosing a name such as;

- The domain name should be relevant to the content on your site
- Make it easy to remember
- Make the domain easy to type
- Keep it as short as possible
- Keep it unique
- Try to avoid using hyphens and numbers
- Avoid infringing any copyright

All of these points above are key to remember when choosing a name. Keeping the name easy to remember and type are probably the top ones as you can have a great name but if it's difficult to type or nobody can remember it then it's no good. We suggest that you avoid using numbers and hyphens because if the user is typing the domain name in on his or her phone they will more than likely have to pause and switch keyboard view to get to the numbers or symbols.

If you are looking for your site to be around for a long period of time, try not to use the latest trends in the name. In 5 or 6 years these trends may not be the latest anymore and that depreciates your name. Using your brand or show name is a great way to associate yourself easily with your podcast, if possible avoid using a name that doesn't relate well to your podcasts name or topic, keeping the name relevant aids in the process of making it easy to remember.

When coming up with ideas layout a sheet of paper or your desired note taking app and just brainstorm ideas. Take a range of keywords and see if any go well together, make sure that any words you do use in the name relate to each other in some way, you can't just go and put random words together and hope it works, for example "potatoraspberry.com" is not a very good name as the words potato and raspberry have no relation to each other, apart from they are both foods.

How do you check if the domain name or names that you have come up with are available? You can use a service such as domajax.com or you can choose to check with a domain name registrar and you can type in a name and it will list what extensions are available. Now you have a name, who do you registrar with? Choosing a domain name registrar is a very simple and easy process as there are many out there. We recommend to stick to some of the well known names such as "GoDaddy", "123-reg.co.uk" or "Namecheap". It is really a case of shopping around to make sure that you get the best price you can.

Podcast Website

Hosting Your Site

After you have chosen and purchased your domain you will then need to think about where you are going to host your website. Web hosting is where you place all of your website files and data. Choosing the right host for you can be a complex and overwhelming task but there are many tools out there to help you.

For most people shared hosting is more than enough to host a website for your podcast. Shared hosting means exactly what it says in the name, it's shared. Your website is hosted on a server somewhere and shared hosting means that you are not the only website on the server, this does not mean that other users of that server will be able to access your files or visa versa. Shared hosting is often a lot cheaper than dedicated hosting for the very reason that they can put a lot of sites on one server. If you are looking to host your podcast files (see the hosting chapter) then you will want to take a look at dedicated hosting services, these are more expensive than shared hosting but offer faster and more reliable services.

Many hosts will advertise "unlimited" plans, these should always be taken with a pinch of salt as they are normally not be truly "unlimited". These will more than likely have a fair usage policy that states if you go over a certain amount of storage or use over a certain amount of bandwidth they are able to terminate your account or take action.

Similar rules apply when choosing a hosting provider in the sense that we recommend that you stick the well known brands such as GoDaddy, BlueHost and HostGator. Avoid choosing a hosting service that you have never heard of before as that is never a good sign, it does not give you reassurance that the company will be around for a long time which means that you will have to end up moving which is never fun. You can search Google for reviews but some of these are often misleading as they are affiliated with the host they are reviewing or they are being sponsored to review it, so naturally they will say good things about it. Shop around and find the best deal possible and avoid getting scammed by poor hosts.

You will want to go with a host that offers a good support system, if you ever do need help with setting up or ever have a problem you want good support to help you. A good trick to finding good support is to test out support before purchasing, you can either try out the email or live chat or by phoning up their support team. You can enquire to them about purchasing hosting but they may be more inclined to provide better support as it may result in a sale then if you are already an existing customer, you may want to try and ask some general support questions and see what there responses are.

Podcast Website

Setting up Your Domain

When you have purchased both your domain and your hosting you will then need to link them together. At first it can seem like a daunting task but we will guide you through the process and try to make it as easy as possible. We will talk about using a service called CloudFlare later in this chapter which adds a couple of steps to this process, take a look at the diagram below to gain an understanding of what you need to do.

We need to point the domain name to the hosting service, to do this you will need to locate the name servers of your hosting service, so you can use them for the domain. Usually the name server details will look along the lines of this;

- ns1.example.com
- ns2.example.com

Some may require you to enter the relevant IP addresses along with the name servers (in the form of a string of numbers separated by dots). You can find out exactly what you need and all of the relevant information by checking your hosting and domain providers support pages, these may vary per host or domain registrar.

Some hosts will require you to add the domain to your account (set the URL, name and password) so that it knows to point to your account. When you have set up the add-on domain if required (see your hosting providers support page for details) you can go ahead and enter the name server information of your hosting provider into your domain registrar.

If you ever have any problems or get stuck during the process then you can ring up your domain name or hosting support teams and they will be more than happy to help you a long the way, some may even offer to do it for you. Don't be afraid to ask them questions, they are there to help so take advantage of that.

CloudFlare

CloudFlare offer a great service that can speed up your site and also up the security on your site. It detects incoming attacks and rejects them, this will reduce the chance of your website getting hacked or broken into. CloudFlare will also save on bandwidth so if you are on a hosting plan that only offers a limited amount of site bandwidth, using CloudFlare will help squeeze that little bit more out of it. CloudFlare offer both a free plan and a pro plan, you can add up to multiple sites to each account, it doesn't matter how many sites you have you can keep track of all of them using just a single account.

Podcast Website

CloudFlare is very easy to set up, they guide you through the process after you have created your account. On the dashboard page you enter your site name (example.com) and then it will attempt to scan for the record of your website (A records and such), after it has detected them it will let you continue on with the setup. It will then ask you to review the DNS records and add any that are missing, if you are not sure on what these are then you can simply click to the next pane as it should have already detected them all. You can then select your plan (free or paid) and then the performance and security of your site, most of the time you can leave them set to the default settings which are normally "CDN only" for performance and "Medium" for security.

The next step is very similar to the way we hooked up the domain to our hosting before, it will give you the new name server settings that you will need to update on your domain registrar. It will give you a list of your current name servers on the left and on the right it lists the ones you need to change them to. If you remember the diagram on the previous page we are trying to get the domain to point to CloudFlare and then CloudFlare to point to our hosting provider. Example;

- ns1.example.com **change to** example.ns.cloudflare.com
- ns2.example.com **change to** example.ns.cloudflare.com
- ns3.example.com Delete this name server

Some hosting providers such as Media Temple allow you to set up CloudFlare directly from your Media Temple control panel as an add-on service.

One thing to remember is that when linking up your domain to your hosting or when setting up CloudFlare is that it will not take immediate effect. Sometimes when you hook a domain name up it can take anywhere up to 48 hours for the name servers to change, be patient.

Installing Software

You can hand code the website yourself but there are many great pieces of software out there to make creating and maintaining your website a breeze. There are three main services plus an additional one we'll look at later. The three main ones are Wordpress, Drupal and Joomla. Wordpress is the biggest of the three but they all offer a very similar look, feel and offer similar functionality. For this chapter we are going to take a look at Wordpress as it is one of the largest and most widely used out there, Wordpress is also free.

All three pieces of the software mentioned above are known as content management systems (CMS). A CMS is a system that allows you to publish, edit and modify content as well as site maintenance from a central page. Wordpress allows you to add individual posts and you can use plugins and themes to customise the look and functionality of your website. You can make your site look very unique and make it stand out from the rest.

Podcast Website

Installing and Setting up Wordpress Manually

A lot of hosting providers offer a one click installer option that will automatically create the database and auto install Wordpress for you. We will look at manually creating the database in case you are using a hosting provider that does not offer the on click install approach.

Step 1

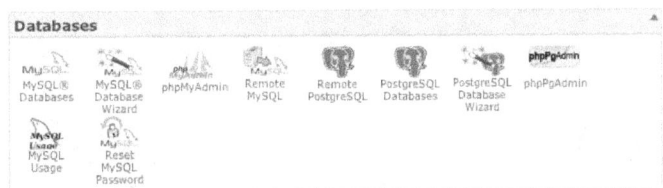

In your hosting control panel you need to locate the databases section. Select MySQL databases, this should then take you to a page where you can add, edit and remove MySQL databases and MySQL users.

Step 2

Enter a short name for your database. An example of a name for a Wordpress database would be "wrdp1", but you can name it whatever you want, don't use spaces or other characters just to keep it simple. In the picture above there is a prefix under the blurred section, this may vary for each hosting service but for this example it would read "example_wrdp1".

Step 3

We then need to create a new user. Under the MySQL Users section add a new user, as you can see the prefix is there again (under the blurred section). It is recommended that you keep your username the same as your database name so you don't forget which one is which if you have multiple ones. When entering a new password make sure to create a strong one as the database is where all of the information is stored, if they provide a password generator use it (keep it over 12 or so characters long) or use "howsecureismypassword.net" to calculate how strong your password is.

Podcast Website

Step 4

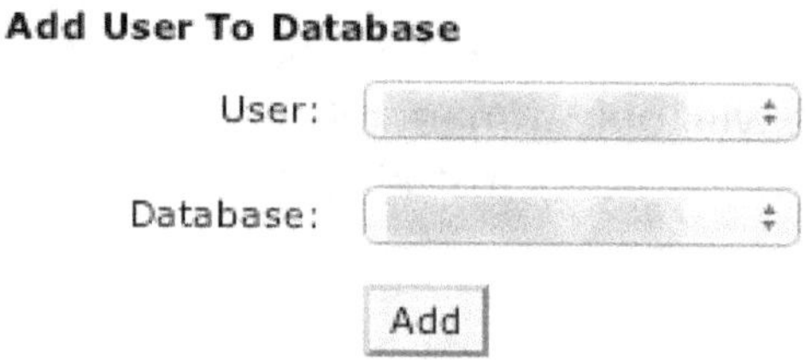

We then need to add the user that we have just created to the database that we have also just created. Navigate to the 'Add User To Database' section and there should be two drop down menus. Under the user one select the user you have just created and under the database one select the database you have just created, then click 'Add'.

Step 5

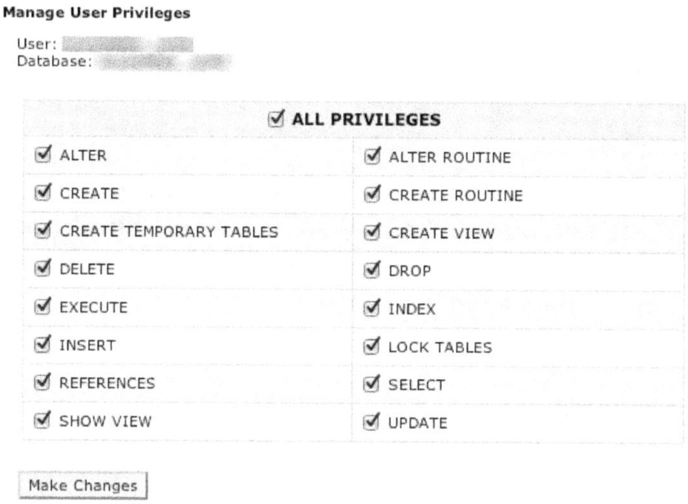

It will then take you to a page asking you what privileges the user should have on that database, select all of them or simply click 'All Privileges'. This will allow the user to add, edit or remove anything in that database which is what we need, as when you write a post for your website it will save it to this database.

Step 6: Setting up Wordpress
Next we need to set up Wordpress manually, you will need to download Wordpress to your computer from wordpress.org. When you have downloaded it proceed to step 7.

Podcast Website

61

Step 7
Upload the Wordpress files that you have just downloaded to your root directory of your website (usually located in the public_html folder OR if you have added it as an add-on domain it may be located under public_html/example.com). To upload your files we recommend that you use a FTP application. You can upload to your host using their built in file manager in your control panel but these can often be temperamental. FileZilla, Transmit, Cyberduck and ForkLift are all good FTP applications. If you need help setting up an FTP connection your host should provide all the details you need to set it up.

Your file directory should look something like the image on the right after it has finished uploading all the Wordpress files.

Name	Size
cgi-bin	--
wp-admin	--
wp-content	--
wp-includes	--
400.shtml	130 bytes
401.shtml	162 bytes
403.shtml	201 bytes
404.shtml	83 bytes
500.php	363 bytes
500.shtml	71 bytes
default.html	Zero KB
favicon.ico	1.1 KB
index.php	395 bytes
license.txt	19.9 KB
readme.html	9.2 KB
wp-activate.php	4.3 KB
wp-app.php	1.4 KB
wp-blog-header.php	271 bytes
wp-comments-post.php	3.5 KB
wp-config-sample.php	3.2 KB
wp-config.php	3.5 KB
wp-cron.php	2.7 KB
wp-links-opml.php	2.0 KB
wp-load.php	2.3 KB
wp-login.php	29.1 KB
wp-mail.php	7.7 KB
wp-pass.php	413 bytes
wp-register.php	334 bytes
wp-settings.php	9.9 KB
wp-signup.php	18.3 KB
wp-trackback.php	3.7 KB
xmlrpc.php	2.8 KB

Step 8
Navigate to your website and you should be greeted with the Wordpress install screen. When asked for details your screen should look something like this (note that some fields may already filled out):

Details

Database Name: example_wrdp1
User Name: example_wrdp1
Password: Password we created for the new user
Database host: Usually 'localhost'
Table prefix: The default is 'wp_'. You can change this to anything you like, it needs to be changed if you want to run multiple Wordpress installs within the same database, it can also be changed as a security measure as it makes your database hard to guess.

For the database name, enter the name of the database you created in step 2 including the prefix if there was one. Do the same for the user created in step 3.

Podcast Website

Step 9
After you have entered all the database details click submit and run the install. You will then be asked for the details of your admin user. Create a username and a strong password as these are the details you will be using to access the Wordpress control panel. Enter the name of your website and a tagline if you have one.

After you have done this and if all has gone correctly then Wordpress has installed and set up fine! You can then navigate to your website and add /wp-admin on the end to get to your Wordpress control panel (example.com/wp-admin).

Using a One-Click Installer to Install Wordpress

If your host has a on-click installer system then it is much easier to install Wordpress along with a wide range of other software.

Step 1

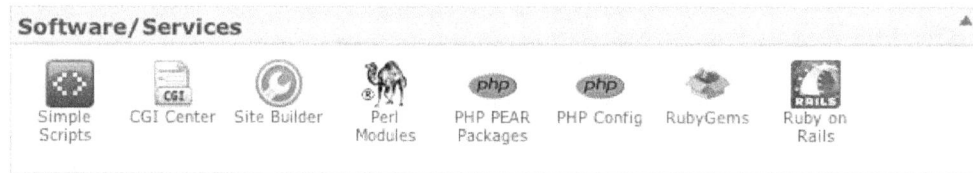

Locate your scripts installer in your hosting control panel

Step 2

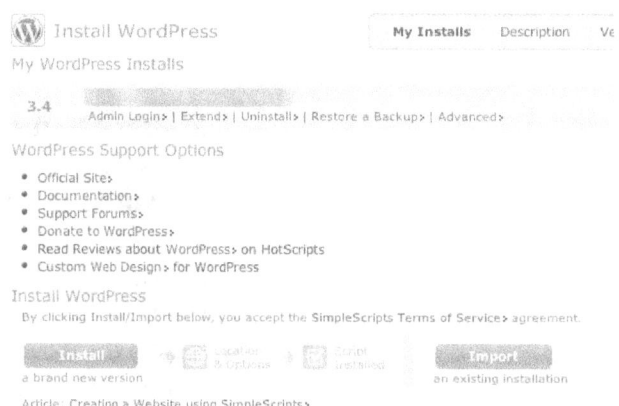

Navigate to the Wordpress install in the software selection. From here you can see any current installations of Wordpress you have and can optionally uninstall them. You can also set up a new Wordpress install (this is what we will be doing) and you can import from a backup you may have.

Podcast Website

Step 3

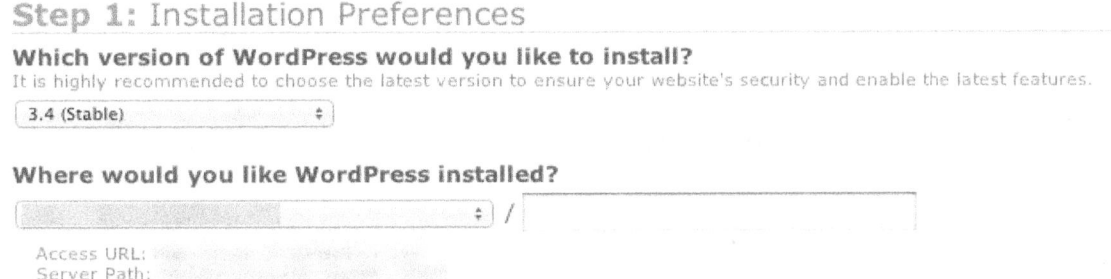

Select the version of Wordpress you want to install, we recommend installing the newest version so you can just leave this option default. Then decide where you want to install it, from the drop down menu you can select the domain name you want to install it on (example.com), you can alternatively select a sub directory to install it in (example.com/example). You can have a Wordpress install in the main directory (example.com) and have one in the sub directory (example.com/example). Both of these installs will be separate from each other.

Step 4

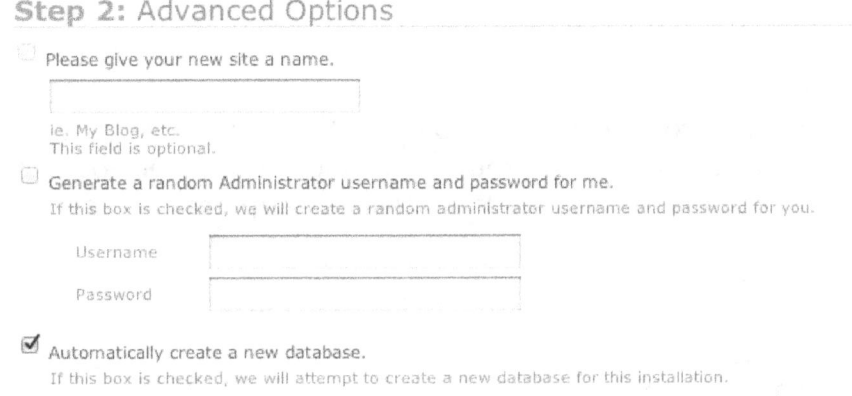

It will then ask you to give your site a name and enter the details for the admin user of the site. There is also an option to automatically create a new database, leave this ticked and it will do it by itself. See the 'Installing Wordpress manually' section of this chapter if you want to create the database manually.

Podcast Website

Step 5

Step 3: Plugins and Themes
We can automatically install additional plugins and themes. You can also browse the library › after installation.

☐ Cashie Commerce by Cashie Commerce ›   ☐ SmallBiz Theme by Expand2Web   ☐ Wiziapp by Wiziapp Solutions Ltd. ›

 Cashie Commerce is the fastest way to start selling on your WordPress site. Integrated with PayPal, it's secure and easy to set up - and you'll incur no fees until you sell.

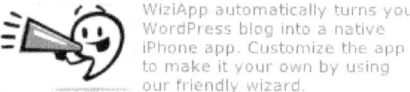 Create your website in minutes including multiple Pages, Blog, Facebook and Mobile!

Activate under Appearance -> Themes.

WiziApp automatically turns your WordPress blog into a native iPhone app. Customize the app to make it your own by using our friendly wizard.

Step 4: Legal Information

☐ I have read the terms and conditions of the GPLv2 license agreement ›

[Complete]

Some automatic installers will try and install some themes and plugins but we recommend that you uncheck all of them if it does offer you them.

Check the terms and conditions and click complete.

Your new Wordpress installation is now ready and waiting! Navigate to your website and put /wp-admin on the end of the address (example.com/wp-admin) and you can then login by entering the details that you created in step 4.

Themes and Plugins

After you have installed Wordpress you'll want to customise it to suit your needs. Wordpress is a very flexible piece of software, you can change pretty much anything you want on your website. There are hundreds of free themes and also many sites that offer quality paid/premium themes.

Sites that offer good quality themes:

- WooThemes (woothemes.com)
- WPZOOM (wpzoom.com)
- Templatic (templatic.com)
- ThemeForest (themeforest.net)

Most of these themes offer you the ability to further edit the theme. If you know your way around HTML, CSS and PHP then you can edit the code. If not, a lot of themes offer a set range of settings so you can adjust and tweak your website.

Podcast Website

Plugins allow you to add extra functionality to your website. Here are some recommendations of plugins that are worth installing.

StatPress

As covered in the tracking statistics chapter, it is important to keep a track of both your podcast downloads and also the number of visitors to your website. Statpress is a great plugin for doing just that. It allows you to get an in depth look at who and how many people are visiting your site.

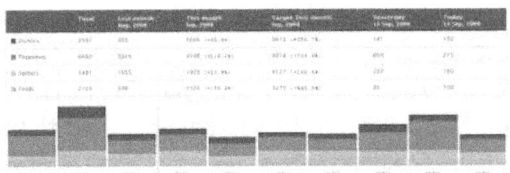

You can view in detail the people who have last visited your site and where they came from. Statpress is a plugin that everyone who is using Wordpress should have as it offers a large number of very useful features.

Pretty Link

Pretty Link is a great plugin that allows you to create new URLs that redirect to different pages. Pretty link enables you to shorten links using your own domain name instead of using services such as bit.ly or tinyurl.com. In addition to creating the links you can also track hits to each URL you create and provides full detail about the hits, similar to Statpress.

Pretty link allows you to clean up links that you can use with affiliates and emails etc. If you send out a newsletter you can see how many people click on a link if you use Pretty Link to create the URLs you include in your newsletter.

For example you may have a link to an episode that is example.com/?p=3453456 - that's not a very clean link and its certainly not memorable, so you may want to change it to example.com/episode12.

WebsiteDefender

WebsiteDefender is a plugin to help you secure your Wordpress installation and it provides detailed reporting on any problems it may discover and will then advise you on how to fix them.

WebsiteDefender includes the ability to backup your Wordpress database if anything goes wrong, remove certain things for non-admins that may be helpful for hackers, ability to change the database prefix and much more. Did we mention that it's free?

All of the plugins mentioned above are free and are must haves for your new Wordpress installation.

Podcast Website

Going Mobile

Mobile is the place to be nowadays, there are many plugins out there that you can install on Wordpress that will add a mobile version of your website. This means that when you or your listeners visit your site on a mobile platform it should auto detect this and change the site to be suitable for mobile viewing. When looking to get a new theme, we recommend that you find one that includes what is called 'responsive design'. Responsive design means that the site changes to work on different devices.

Adding Audio and Video to Posts

PowerPress is a plugin that allows you to easily add both audio and video to your posts by adding a line of code in your post, when you add this line the end result is a video or audio player depending on what the file you added is. You can customise both the audio and video players so you can change them to suit the look of your site.

Distribution

Chapter Summary

Distributing your podcast is important — this is the process of putting it out there for people to hear!

There are many places online where you can post your podcast episodes, such as your podcast website as well as the iTunes Store, Zune and Podcast directories. There are hundreds of other services, we'll take a look at some of the main ones and how to get your podcast on them.

Summary

Having your podcast on as many sites and services is key to building a bigger and more versatile listener or viewer base. Services such as the iTunes Store and Zune allow you to submit your podcast for free, so why wouldn't you submit your show?

RSS

Before you can submit your show to iTunes, Zune and the like you will need to setup an RSS feed for your show episodes. RSS, otherwise known as "Rich Site Summary" or "Really Simple Syndication" is what is used by "podcatching" software such as iTunes and Zune. An RSS file/document is known as a "feed". It keeps information such as the title of that "entry", the date it was posted, the link to the audio/video file etc.

Setting an RSS feed up is extremely simple! You can of course do it manually, although this requires some coding knowledge. However, there are many applications that will set one up without any coding knowledge.

Mac OS X - A good RSS creator/updater for Mac is "Feeder". The application costs £27 ($39). It allows you to create and publish an RSS feed easily and quickly.

Windows - FeedForAll is a good option. It has the same basic principles as Feeder, the only difference being that it's for Windows. It runs around £26 ($39).

When creating your RSS feed, you will have to enter various details about your podcast such as the name of it, a description, author etc. Most of this information will be used by iTunes, Zune and other podcatching software which will use the RSS feed to retrieve information about your show. Once you've created an RSS feed you'll need to upload it, you can use your website host. It's an extremely small file, so space isn't an issue. Both apps mentioned above will allow you to upload your RSS file straight from the app after entering some FTP information about your hosting account. This information can be found in your hosting "dashboard".

Did you know?

Apple added podcast support to iTunes in June 2005, at the time, iTunes was in version 4.9.

Distribution

Incase you're unsure, the RSS feed does not host your podcast audio/video file(s), it simply includes a link to where these files are located, so when the podcast catching software (such as iTunes or Zune) "contacts" the feed, it knows where to download the episode from. If you're still unsure on how RSS works, see the diagram below.

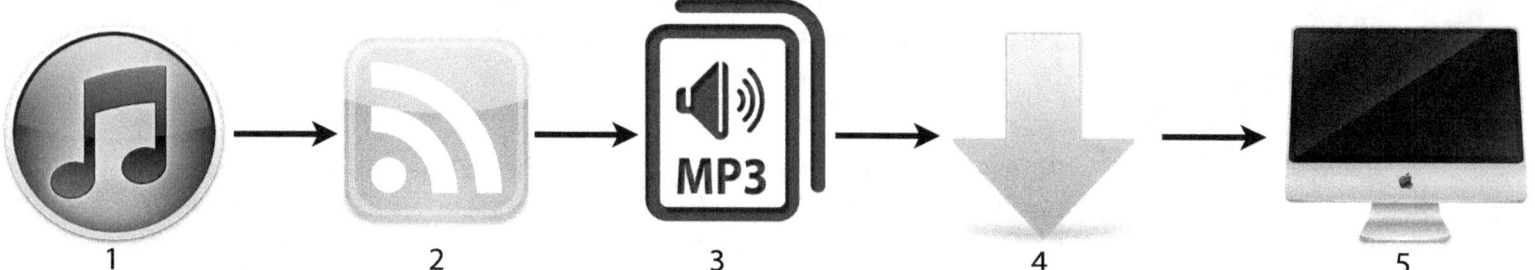

1. Podcatching software (such as iTunes and Zune) reaches out to the RSS feed.
2. The RSS feed then directs the software to the audio or video file, this information (including a link to the audio/video file) is "embedded" within the RSS entries (each episode has it's own, entry).
3. The audio/video file is then accessed by the podcatching software.
4. The episode's file is downloaded.
5. The file finishes downloading, and is ready to be listened to.

Once you've created your RSS feed, you should "verify" it to make sure that it's readable and that there are no errors. An easy way to do this is by searching for "RSS Feed Validator" on Google. Once you've made sure your feed doesn't have any errors, you can now submit your feed to iTunes, Zune etc.

iTunes

iTunes was one of the first main services to adopt podcasting. In fact, some would say Apple's iTunes is one of the main factors that kicked off the era of podcasting. Submitting your podcast to iTunes is completely free, takes no time and obviously helps with the discovery of your podcast.

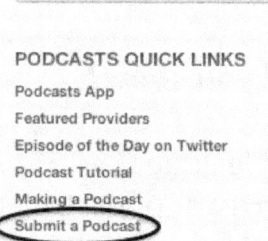

Once you have created your RSS feed, make sure you have something published on it. It can be an audio file with a quick announcement about your show. It can be a 10 second clip, just make sure something is on the feed. Sometimes podcasts are rejected because the feed is empty, because it cannot be confirmed whether it is working or not.

After making sure you have something on the RSS feed, you can submit your show to iTunes, to do this, open iTunes on your computer, open the iTunes Store and go to the Podcasts section.

In the right hand side of the Podcasts section, there will be a menu titled "Podcasts Quick Links", at the bottom you'll see "Submit a Podcast". Click this link.

Distribution 69

Enter the link to the RSS feed which you have already created, the link should end with either the extension ".rss" or ".xml", both are recognised by iTunes, and other podcatching software.

An example for your RSS link would be "http://mysite.com/mypodcastname.xml"

Once you have entered your RSS link, simply hit "Continue". You have now successfully submitted your podcast to the iTunes Store. You should receive an email from Apple confirming your submission, and then another email to say that it has been accepted (this can take a number of days). There are occasions when podcasts are denied, but the\se are normally due to a broken RSS link or other factors which may be violating iTune's terms of service.

Zune/Windows Phone

Zune is Microsoft's own "iTunes" which also has a podcast directory. It has a pretty similar procedure when it comes to submitting your podcast. At the time of writing, Zune is changing coherent to the new system using Windows 8 and Windows Phone 8. While you can use Zune's own software to submit your podcast, you must have a Windows 7 machine to do so.

The simplest, and easiest way to submit your podcast to the Zune catalogue, is to email or tweet Rob Greenlee, the content manager at Zune. Rob's email is "v-robgr@microsoft.com". Alternatively, you can tweet him "@robgreenlee" and ask him to add your podcast to the catalogue.

Website

Having a website for your podcast is crucial! If you're wanting to know about making a website for your podcast, posting your episodes on the website and more, check out the "Website" chapter in the book. Your website is the place to direct your listeners to find show notes, other episodes and other content you may be producing. This is important as it means there is a central location for all of your content instead of multiple locations with only some content on each.

Podcast Directories

There are hundreds, if not thousands of podcast directories online which are free to submit your podcast to! Search online "podcast directory" and you'll be sure to find some, make sure to submit your podcast to these because after all, it's free promotion for your show!

Tracking Statistics

Chapter Summary

In this chapter we will be taking a look at why you want to track the statistics of your show. Ever wondered how many people download each episode? How many people download your show? Where are your most listeners are from?

We'll cover a range of services for tracking your downloads and a range of other things.

Summary

Sometimes it is very useful to know how many people download each episode of your show, how many people are subscribed to your show and where your listeners are in the world. All of this information is not just useful for you but it is also useful if you want to talk to potential advertisers or sponsors.

Why and Why Not?

There are many reasons why you should and even some for why you shouldn't look at your statistics. Keeping track of your statistics is very helpful if you ever do look into getting in contact with potential sponsors or advertisers as statistics is something they will ask for.

Start tracking as early as you can, this helps when you want look at trends for your show (what months performed well? What did you do differently in those months?) There is no point starting to track a week before you get in contact with a sponsor as that does not give you enough time to get trend information about your show. Sponsors will want to know as much as possible about your shows statistics so they know when and where to advertise.

One thing to be warned about though is looking at your statistics too often. This can often leave you to be unhappy about your shows performance because maybe the numbers are not what you want them to be. Remember that even if only one person is subscribed to your show, they are interested in what you are saying and if they enjoy it they will spread the word about your show online and to their friends.

What do we mean when we use the word '**trends**'? A trend in stats is much like a trend in real life. You may use graphs at work to show different trends in profit for different months etc. You may use trends to see what worked and what didn't work. This is the same for viewing trends in your podcast statistics.

If you are a business then you can see different statistics for different campaigns you ran on your podcast. You'll be able to see what worked and when it worked, so if you run a new segment on your show then you may be able to see that reflected in your stats. If you ran an advert on a site or something then you can see that reflected in your stats, what kind of impact did it have on your downloads?

Did you know?

It took the web only 5 years to reach 50 million users whereas it took radio 38 years to reach 50 million listeners.

Tracking Statistics

Services

When looking for a service to track statistics you want to keep in mind a few things:

- Does it allow you to see the demographic of your listeners/viewers? i.e. Where your listeners are from?
- Does it list individual episodes?
- Does it allow you to view trends of your shows?

Being able to see where your listeners are from in the world is very valuable information, it allows to target your audience specific information depending on where they are from.

It tends to be that the service you use to host your shows statistics may be more accurate than using a third party service. This does not mean that you should not use a third party service but it is recommended that you use your hosting services built in options. Libsyn, for example offer some great options for viewing your statistics visually.

Podtrac

Podtrac offer a fantastic service for both publishers and advertisers. If you are a podcaster (a publisher) then Podtrac offers you the ability to view nice, easy to visually interpret reports about your shows and individual episodes. You can view the download statistics by episode, by source or by country which allows you to gain the most information about where your listeners are from and what device they are listening/watching from.

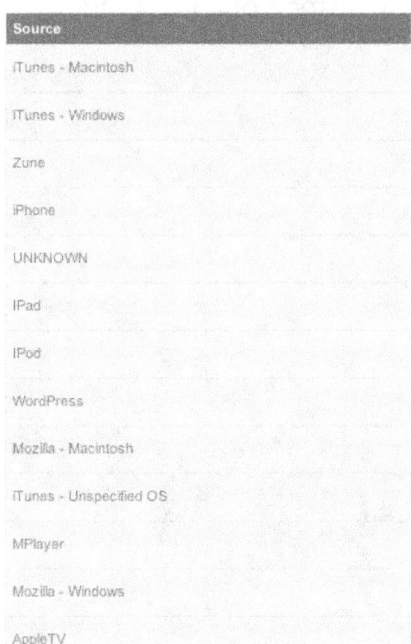

Being able to view the source is very useful, it allows you to see what most people are listening/watching on. This means that you can see where you need to improve, if your mobile subscribers are very low then you may be in need of improving the mobile experience, such as acquiring an app or getting a new mobile site.

If you are an advertiser then Podtrac also offers a great service, Podtrac is not only for content creators but also for people or businesses who are looking to advertise on a podcast. This allows advertisers to get in contact with publishers and vice versa.

Tracking Statistics

Libsyn

Libsyn are most widely known for their podcast hosting services but along with that comes a great statistics service. The statistics section is built into the hosting side so you can only use it if you host your podcast with Libsyn.

Libsyn offer a great way to view your podcast statistics visually, you can view very intricate details about each episode which can be very useful. You can order statistics of each episode in ascending or descending order, which allows you to see which episodes have been downloaded the most (you can also do this for individual months). You can then use this information to work out what you did on those episodes that made them so good and you can try to replicate it.

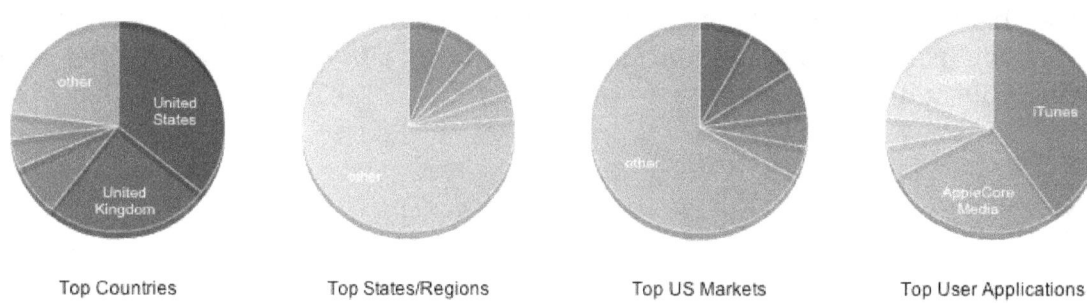

Top Countries · Top States/Regions · Top US Markets · Top User Applications

Libsyn offer an in depth look at your statistics and where your subscribers are listening from. It allows you to select a certain time frame, for example if you wanted to look at how many downloads you had between April and June. It also allows you to view other useful and interesting data such as the top countries in which people download your show and the top applications that are used to listen to or watch your show.

Libsyn displays all of the information in a visual and easy to understand manor, instead of it just being a load of unordered numbers on a page.

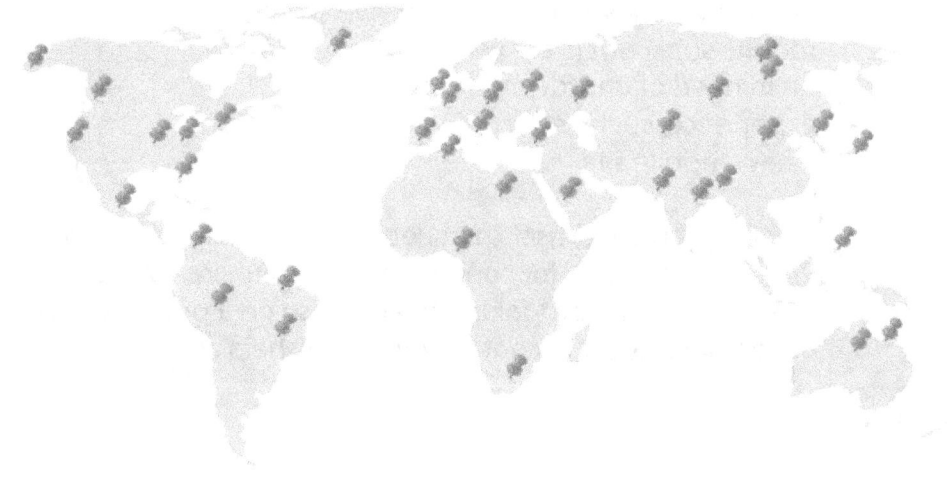

Tracking Statistics

Website Statistics

Tracking statistics doesn't just mean tracking how many people download your show, but also how many people are visiting your site. Very similar rules apply to the website stats tracking such as looking at trends, country specific data and much more.

Statistics can also be used for working out what adverts to display on your site. If your sites referrers are mostly from technology sites then you want to display technology ads to those people, but if your referrers are mostly people from fashion websites then you should display fashion ads. By adding the correct adverts on your website, you will likely earn more money because the people are more likely to click on them, as you're reaching your targeted audience, instead of a generalised market.

Being able to see what countries your users are from can be used to your advantage as well, you can adjust your content accordingly to the biggest countries and you can add country specific ads.

If you are a business running a social media campaign you will be able to see the impact of that campaign in your statistics, which social network brought you in the most users? What time of day you should post on the social networks to get the most reach?

All this information can be useful to you in a number of different ways, use this information to your advantage, to improve your content and to improve the way you share your content.

Statpress

If you are using Wordpress for your website then you can use the free plugin, Statpress. Statpress is one of the best plugins as it offers the most features and is very accurate. It sets out targets based on previous months that it believes you should get for the current month, based on your previous month's statistics. Another useful thing that it does is that it separates the spiders (Google, Yahoo etc) from your "`human" visitors, so you are able to get an accurate representation of how many visitors you actually have.

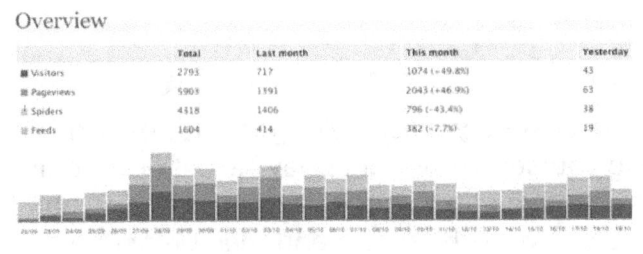

Google Analytics

If you are not using Wordpress (or even if you are) you can use Google's service. Google offer a tracking service called Google analytics, you can track multiple sites under one account.

You can view real-time data i.e. how many people are on your site at the current moment. Another good feature Google Analytics offers is the ability to find out how many of your visitors are new visitors and how many are returning visitors, you can also see the average time someone spends on your site.

Promotion

Chapter Summary

In this chapter we will be covering how to promote your show. Whether it's via social media, adverts or your website.

This chapter will cover the best ways to promote your show, including some tips on reaching the most people possible. It's not just about where, but also when. Getting the timing right is crucial for promoting your show.

Summary

So you've just posted your first show and now you want to tell people about it? There are many places you can post to, social networks, a newsletter and feature it on your website although possibly the most powerful is word of mouth.

Social Media

Social media is a term for all sites that provide different social actions. For example, Twitter is for short updates whereas Facebook is a full blown social network for sharing updates, photos, joining events and other activities.

One of the best ways of promoting your show is via social media. As of writing this book Facebook has over 1 billion users and Twitter has well over 500 million users. Just by those numbers you can tell that it is important to reach people on those networks, obviously you will never reach everyone, but there will be an audience for your genre of show. Always remember, there will be someone new who is interested in your show.

Most of these services are free so why not utilise them? Creating a Twitter account is free and super simple, setting up a Facebook and Google+ page is also super simple and again, free.

Social Media: How Does It Help?

If you are posting your show on your iTunes and expecting people to magically find it then you are kidding yourself. iTunes does have a half decent discovery system but people are not likely to discover your show if you don't them about it. Tweeting about it, posting it on Facebook etc. all help in the discovery of your show, as mentioned before getting your podcast discovered is one of the hardest parts about having a podcast.

If you have a Twitter account and some followers then why not tweet when you upload a new episode? When you Tweet you are telling people who may never have found out about your show that you have uploaded a new episode, the same goes for posting it on Facebook etc.

Did you know?

Twitter users welcomed 2013 with up to 33,388 Tweets per second, which was more than double the previous years.

Promotion

Case Study: Starbucks

Create your however-you-want-it Frappuccino®

Lets take a look at Starbucks and the way they are using social media to help promote their "Frappuccino Happy Hour" campaign.

What is their aim?
They're setting photo challenges everyday for 12 days in which people have to take a photo with their Starbucks Frappuccino in a different way everyday. They will give a £10 Starbucks card out everyday to the winner of that days photo contest

How are they using social media for this and how is it benefitting their brand?
They are getting people to upload the photos either via Instagram or Twitter and tag them with the hashtag #MyFrappuccino. Each day the new challenge is posted on Twitter with a link to the contest. Every time someone posts a photo all their friends will see it and see what it is, this is free advertising for Starbucks.

The incentive for people to enter the contest is the reward card.

Promotion

As we have seen from Starbucks campaign using social media can be a massive advantage, but it is no good if you are not using it correctly. You need to make sure you are targeting the correct things to the correct audience.

The next question is when and how often should I post?

Your followers and friends do not want to hear about your new podcast episode all day, everyday for the next week. Learn when enough is enough. If your show is a weekly show then the best times to post are on the day you release the episode then a few times throughout the week. If you post every hour of every day then the people following you will more than likely either unfollow you or ignore your content.

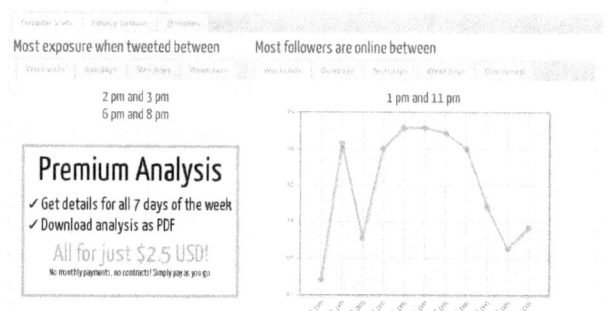

Post when you think your followers and friends are most active, if you post during the middle of the day on weekday then they are most likely at work and are not going to be able to listen or watch it. You can use a service such as 'Tweriod' to work out when your followers are most active.

Another thing to remember when posting is to take into account different timezones. If you are in the UK and you post about your new episode at 10AM that means that when you post it will be 5AM in the USA (ET), if you do not check timezones then some people may miss it. We have covered in the 'Tracking Stats' chapter about finding out what countries your subscribers are in. A good timezone converter is worldtimebuddy.com. It allows you to easily add different locations and then see the time in multiple geographic locations compared to your country/city.

Another thing to consider, is instead of just saying on your post "a new episode is up at...", make it appealing, mention what you discussed, i.e. "in this week's episode we talk about..." - this will make your audience aware of what you talked about, and may make it seem more of an incentive to listen.

Promotion

Newsletter

Another way of promoting your show is by creating a newsletter. Do not underestimate the power of a newsletter, email is often considered as a very personal means of communication (well, as personal as talking over the Internet can be). Email is something personal and we treat it much like our phone number, very private and to our close friends. So if someone signs up to your newsletter it will get delivered directly to their inbox.

You can create a newsletter to update people on what new episodes you have, any changes or updates in your life or to do with the podcast. You can make the newsletter very personal, as we spoke about earlier in this section that email is very personal. You can make it personal by including such things as updates in your life and generally making it more of a chat than a formal newsletter. Some services allow you to automatically include peoples names (if they have entered it) which adds to the personal touch. Don't fill up peoples inbox, would you like it if someone constantly kept sending you emails every day? Unless you have something major to say then sending a newsletter once every couple of weeks or even once a month is more than adequate.

How do you get people to subscribe to your newsletter?
One of the best ways to get people to subscribe to your newsletter is by offering them something in return. One of the things that some people offer is special deals in the newsletter, so if someone subscribes to the newsletter in the next newsletter they will receive a discount on something, saving money is something everyone wants to do. Some people also offer an eBook in return, if you make an eBook or a similar item then you could offer that in return for subscribing to your newsletter. You can include a welcome message to new subscribers. Whenever someone signs up they get a friendly welcome message, in which you could include something like a link to download your eBook or a discount as mentioned earlier.

Newsletter Services

Tinyletter
Tinyletter offer a good service for a very simple newsletter, Tinyletter allows you to create very basic newsletters and sign up pages to go along with it. It allows you to see basic statistics of who has read your email out of your subscribers, which can be useful.

Mailchimp
Mailchimp offer another great service but this time with a large platoon of features. They offer great statistics, multiple email campaigns and some really high quality templates for your newsletters.

Promotion

Aweber

Aweber is considered to be one of the titans of the email marketing industry. It offers many of the same features as some of the others do plus more. Aweber does not offer a free plan, whereas both Mailchimp and Tinyletter do.

Word of Mouth

The best way to get new people to listen or watch your show is by word of mouth. Someone is more likely to search for something if they are told it by a friend or colleague rather than if they find it on the web. We trust the information from a friend or colleague more than we will on the web. If you get people talking about your show then word will get around quicker.

Featuring Episodes On Your Website

If your podcast has a website or even if you have a personal website or blog, you can post to these. As covered in the 'Podcast Website' chapter, having a website for your podcast can be a vital tool. You can post new episodes to the site and direct people to your website meaning they will be able to browse all of your content all in one place.

Tag Your Episodes

Tags are great for generating traffic! Search engines use tags to help generate meaningful search results. You can add tags to your episode posts on Wordpress, and other blogging platforms. When tagging, make sure to include keywords of what you've discussed or talked about on the episode. For example, if you're talking about computers, tag "computers", and if you were talking about specific makes or models, tag those as well. This means people who search for those terms are more likely to find your podcast.

Interview Interesting People

Interviewing "pioneers" or "market leaders" in your niche is a fantastic way not only to make your show more interesting, but also to generate traffic. Many people will share the interview online and therefore their audience and followers will be introduced to your podcast, some of which may subscribe.

Get Listed in Podcast Directories

Search for "podcast directory" and you'll find thousands of results. Make sure to add your podcast to some of these directories, by doing this you're increasing the amount of exposure your podcast is getting, which can only be a good thing!

Monetisation

Chapter Summary

Many podcasters make a living from podcasting, and although this isn't normally the case, it is still possible to make money from podcasting.

Monetising your show isn't an easy task, and you shouldn't start a podcast with this being your main target. However, there are ways to earn money from podcasting which we'll cover.

Summary

Podcasting for the majority is a hobby, and nothing more. However, it is possible to make money from it. You shouldn't create a podcast with the intention of this. Earning money is a bonus that doesn't always happen.

It Takes Time

If your show is going to be profitable, don't expect it to happen overnight! It takes a lot of time, effort and dedication to make money. There are many ways of doing it, and some may work better than others.

Affiliates

Many online stores and services will offer an affiliate program. The idea being, that you signup for it and recommend the service to your listeners, directing them to a link that is custom to you. Every time someone signs up or buys something using the link you have provided, you will earn a certain percentage of the product's price. A general rule to follow is to only use affiliate programs of the services that you personally use, or trust and feel comfortable recommending. Don't recommend a service that you wouldn't personally use. Remember, you're recommending this service to an audience that has built up trust in you, don't break that trust by recommending the first service that you can think of! A lot of services you currently use already have an affiliate program, so why not use the services you already know, have tried and can recommend knowing that they're trustworthy and worthy of your recommendation. Affiliate marketing can bring a lot of profit in for people, and is known as a "passive" income strategy, this means that your input isn't required, and that you can literally make money as you sleep! This is probably one of the easiest methods of potentially earning an income, as there are no requirements for it, as long as you have people to recommend the service to, and a good service to recommend!

Did you know?

It is said that the fast growing podcast advertising market surpassed £254 million ($400 million) in 2011!

Monetisation

Sponsors/Advertisers

Sponsors are attained by reaching out to companies and explaining what you're after, and why you feel it would be beneficial to both the company and your podcast. Quoting prices can be a tricky thing to do, it all depend on your show's figures and it is something that depends on numerous factors. Don't overprice, but don't underprice. Also, be honest with the company on your show's figures. If a company rejects your request, don't be put off! You may get rejected over and over, this is normal. It isn't something every company will welcome with open arms, but if you don't try, you don't get.

Another thing to consider is which companies to reach out to, make sure they are related to the subject of your podcast, otherwise, what is the point of them sponsoring you? Sponsorships can be a hard and strenuous task, that even the best podcasts can struggle with. Some companies may not want to invest money in new media, as they may be more comfortable with current media such as television, radio and online website advertising, as this offers more of a guarantee of results.

Merchandise

Selling merchandise is another great way of earning money from your podcasting efforts. There are many services that will allow you to open an online shop and place your logo on products such as t-shirts, mugs, clocks, mouse mats and more. With no expense to you!

The products are printed and shipped by the company, meaning no effort is required on your behalf after deciding what products to sell, and designing them! You can also set a markup on them, so you can earn profits from the products you're selling. Two examples of companies that allow you to do this are "cafepress.com" and "spreadshirt.com".

More on Sponsors/Advertisers

Although they can be difficult to get, there are advantages of having them, and there are certain things that are useful to know when contacting companies, which we'll cover.

The first thing, is that advertising is easier for podcasters than it is for traditional media as overhead is lower and thus podcasters can run fewer commercials and still break even or even make a profit.

Monetisation

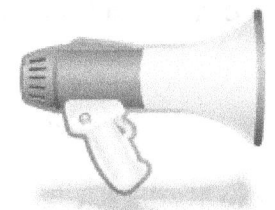

Podcasting is a very unique media when it comes to advertising, as you're talking to a niche market. Compared to television or radio which has a very generalised market. This means that adverts on television and radio will only interest about 1-10% of the audience compared to podcasting which will interest nearly 100% because the advert is related to the content, meaning you're talking to a targeted market. This can be very appealing to a company, so it may be useful to point this out when contacting them. This is a huge advantage because the advert will be appealing to the audience as they're interested in the topic the advert is on, compared to traditional media which is a different case, this also reduces the "annoyance factor" of the advert, which in turn makes it more likely that the audience will pay attention to the advert. The advert is also less of unrelated, annoying interruption and more of a valuable piece of information that is of interest to every single listener.

This is great for the advertiser as they know every penny spent will reach the target audience and will not be wasted in a shotgun approach to marketing. It's great for you the podcaster as it now acts as a gateway to a valuable audience that can be utilised in literally hundreds of ways.

Listeners will generally respond better to your sponsor message when you ask them personally to do so! Letting them know that the sponsors keep the content free will remind them to visit the sponsor's website and buy their products whenever possible.

Advertising Services or Self Selling?

Once you've made the decision to sell sponsorships in your podcast, the question is then "do I use one of the many advertising services to get sponsorships or do I sell my own?" There are advantages and disadvantages to both, and we'll take a look at them.

Ad Networks

If you have a website or blog, you may already have tried ad services, such as Google Adsense, where Google acts as your salesperson, attracting advertisers to the search engine and network of millions of websites and blogs that show the ads and receive a small portion of what the advertiser has paid.

The only problem with this, is that although you only have to paste some HTML code into your website, you may also find out that the service generates just a few pounds/dollars each month. In fact, it may generate so little that it's just not worth giving the ads the space they are taking up on the site at all.

Self Selling

Although more work is required, more profit can be made. This is because you can select a fixed rate for the advert per month. You can sell the adverts on both your website and podcast and you can have flexibility in what is placed on your site. The only problem, is finding companies that are willing to advertise. Although, remember that it's worth pointing out that you already have a niche market, so the advert is appealing to every audience member you have! If you already have contacts and connections in the industry subject you are covering in your podcast, pitch to those people first and work your way out from there.

Monetisation

In order to sell sponsorships, you should have two things:

1. A media kit
2. An advertising agreement

The Media Kit
A media kit tells the advertiser what your show is about, who listens and why they should advertise with you, it could nearly be called your "pitch". It also outlines the various choices the advertiser has when it comes to advertising on both your website and podcast. Media buyers and marketing managers are used to asking for information packaged this way, so having a media kit will show you are serious about your content and that you are conducting your podcast as a true media business. Magazines, radio and websites have been using media kits for many years to attract businesses and showcase their properties to prospects in a positive way.

The media kit doesn't have to be long, in fact, it should only be 2-3 pages maximum. Marketing managers are inundated with sales pitches on a daily basis from media properties who want them to advertise. Keep your information short and to the point and the person you are pitching to will appreciate that you have not wasted their time. Get to the point, but make sure to give them all of the information they need to make a decision.

The media kit should include four sections:

1. **Introduction to the podcast**: This gives the advertiser general information about your show including it's frequency, topics covered and the format (interviews, stories etc.)
2. **Your competitive edge**: This should discuss how you reach out to your listeners and grow, why your show is different from other media and from other podcasts in the same market and why they should spend money on you opposed to or in addition to their existing marketing efforts.
3. **Listener/Viewer demographics**: This should tell the advertiser who your audience is and why they want to listen. If you have not already surveyed your audience, this is the reason to do it now. There are several good web-based surveying tools available such as "SurveyMonkey.com". Advertisers will want to know more about your listeners than just how much money they make and where they live. Ideally, include no less than five but no more than ten questions - this means that more people are likely to respond to your survey as they're not bombarded with questions. The survey will allow the potential advertiser to learn more about your audience and if they're suited for their products and services.
4. **Advertising Rates**: This tells the advertiser how much a sponsorship costs and what is included in each ad buy. List out very clearly what they will be getting for their investment.

What to Sell?
Websites with text content will typically offer a buffet of choice when it comes to advertising and sponsorship. A variety of different banner sizes and placement on the page, each with a different price. This is certainly a legitimate way to offer advertising on your podcast.

Monetisation

An advertiser could choose to just have a banner on the sidebar of your site, while another could choose to purchase a host read 20-second pitch for the advertiser's product or service.

However, this route isn't always of interest to the advertiser. Many choices may seem like a good idea, and it may seem like the more choice you offer the more chance you have of getting the advertiser saying "yes". This list of choice can be overwhelming and sometimes confusing to the reader, meaning advertisers will contemplate on whether to go with a banner, text ad or an audio mention.

A better way of capturing the attention of the advertiser is to offer a single sponsorship for a single episode for a set rate per show, with a minimum buy of a certain number of shows. This means that there is only one choice to make, to buy or not!

Another appealing value advertisers are looking for is exclusivity - not having to share the attention of your audience with any competitors. An example of a show sponsorship would be:

- A 20-second host delivered audio mention of the advertiser's special offer to be run within a set amount of time on the podcast (e.g. within the first 120 seconds, 5 minutes etc.)
- A product mention and thank you at the end of the show.
- A 200 x 33 logo on the homepage, in the sidebar.
- A logo or hotlink in the podcast RSS feed.
- A link or mention in an edition of the newsletter.
- Social Media Mentions on your show's pages.

You can also offer a single sponsor per show for a higher price, meaning you are able to greatly increase the value to the advertiser and respect your listeners by not overwhelming them with advertisements. This also means that there will be a higher percentage of click-through and sales for the sponsor products and services - because there only is one advert for your audience to look at.

Pricing your Podcast Sponsorship
Deciding what to charge is a very difficult thing to do, and there is no set "recipe" for doing it. There are, however, some general things to consider.

The first thing to consider is the cost per thousand (CPM) model of determining banner advertising. CPM was used early on with websites to standardise for advertisers what they were paying for banner ads. For every one thousand times a banner ad was viewed, the advertiser would pay, for example, £10 ($15). The CPM was £10 and the advertiser could then budget how much they wanted to spend. For example, if company A had a budget of £20 and the website offered a CPM of £10, the advertisers banner would be loaded two thousand times. Clicks on the banner were tracked, although the cost was the same no matter how many (or few) times a user clicked on the banner. CPM works for many sites because the demographic range of age, income, location etc. are so wide that it is impossible to target a specific group. Advertisers pay the requested CPM and hope that the audience they are hoping to target will click.

Monetisation

For websites and podcasts with highly targeted and niche content, the audience is targeted and niche. Think about it, if your site only received ten visitors per month, you'd never be able to collect enough money on a CPM model to make it worthwhile. There's just not enough traffic to make the numbers work.

But now imagine that those visitors are extremely well known in the market that your podcast is in, in fact, celebrities in that market - how much would advertisers pay you now to get in front of them? It's an extreme example, but the point is that people need to stop thinking in terms of quantity and start thinking about quality.

If for example, you charge £500 per episode and you have 5000 downloads per show, this works out to a CPM of £100! So, why if a CPM advert would only cost £10 per thousand, would your show cost £100 per thousand? The answer is, because your audience is 100% the target audience, while a CPM model only has about 1% of the target audience.

The true answer to the "what should I charge" question lies in the value of the audience you have. The more difficult it is to reach the audience by other means, the more you can charge advertisers to reach them through your show.

Finally, like everything else in business, start with a figure you believe the market will bear and then negotiate from there if you need to.

The Advertising Agreement and Insertion Order
Once you have an advertiser on board, they're probably going to ask you for an insertion order (IO). The IO contains a few legal items to protect you and also outlines payment terms and what type of "creative" such as banner ads and logos you'll need to fulfil the sponsorship.

Having an agreement and IO for the advertiser to sign will again show you're a professional media property using the right tools to protect both you and the advertiser. It also puts in writing what exactly is expected of you so you can fulfil all of the obligations you have promised to do.

An advantage to offering one package with multiple places of exposure (audio, website, newsletter, RSS etc.) is that more people will see the advert, it will seem more appealing to the advertiser and there will then be more chance of the advertiser renewing after the amount of adverts they have bought have ran out. In other words, pile on as much exposure you can and you'll have an easier time renewing with that advertiser.

Podcasting for Businesses

Chapter Summary

Many businesses are beginning to adopt podcasts due to the fantastic versatility. Podcasts not only allow you to spread the word about a topic, but also a business!

If your business is not podcasting, it is losing out on a fantastic opportunity - for many reasons! We'll take a look at why you should be podcasting, and what it can do for your business.

Summary

Podcasting is essential to businesses of any industry and niche, and because it is a newer form of media, most businesses haven't yet adopted it. Which is why it is a perfect time for your business to be an early adopter!

Reasons

It's simple, podcasting can be on any subject. Meaning, it is compatible with virtually any business. There are many reasons for starting a podcast for your business, but here are just a few:

- Increase your marketing reach and online visibility
- Improve your sales and conversion rates
- Regular line of communication with subscribed listeners
- Value added content increases royalty
- Industry news and trends sets you apart from the competition
- Interviews with leaders in your particular industry/niche will establish your business as a respected leader

These reasons are appealing to any business, though matter what industry it specialises in. A podcast can be used to advertise, to do market research and of course - connect with your customers.
Podcasting isn't just about advertising, in order to make your podcast appealing - you should offer an incentive for your customers to listen. Such as a discount coupon (if applicable), exclusive interviews, competitions etc. You can also focus on many parts of the business to make it appealing to as many people as possible, narrowing down on one part may limit the amount of listeners the show receives.

Did you know?

Many nationwide businesses have started their own podcasts, such as Southwest Airlines, HP and Coca-Cola.

Podcasting for Businesses

Internal Communications

Every business, large or small, has a certain degree of internal communications. Human Resources needs to keep employees up to date on the latest information, facts and figures, news from the CEO etc. Traditionally, this sort of information goes out in the form of newsletter, email or interoffice memo. The information usually is read because it is required somehow - an employee is unlikely to disregard an email regarding changes to the payroll system. However, there's no guarantee the information will be accessed in a timely fashion, and it's extremely difficult to track. This is where podcasts come in.

Southwest Airlines

Podcasts such as the ones that Southwest Airlines put out are an effective way of driving home the mission and core values of a corporation. In having upper management speak to the employees, it reinforces their goals and can even inspire and motivate by generating a sense of camaraderie. Using podcasts has a humanising effect on the dissemination of corporate information, offering a voice instead of the written word.

Not only that, but creating a podcast is a much easier way for a CEO or upper level manager to get a message out than blogging or emailing. Both blogging and emails require time at a keyboard, carefully constructing the message so as to not lose any impact. Communicating in this way can be time consuming, particularly if it is to be something that is updated frequently.

Internal communications, when used effectively, not only inform but also make the employee base a more cohesive, functioning team. Over usage of existing mediums such as email and print newsletters have lost some of their edge in bringing information to employees. Most often than not, the information can go unread. Podcasts offer a way to circumvent the norm and create a new opportunity to communicate with employees and move them toward a common objective.

Hewlett Packard

Hewlett Packard has produced a wide range or podcasts available on their website. The links are found on their news page, a prime location for public relations traffic. Information available ranges from digital photography and image printing to HP's history and tips for small to medium sized businesses. The variety of this information appeals to many different markets, some which may overlap, however, at the core of the podcasts is an attempt to connect with individuals who own or work within small or medium sized businesses.

Podcasting for Businesses

Many of these podcasts are related to new products and the benefits that are delivered to the consumer by using them.

Branding, Marketing, Advertising

Perhaps one of the most exciting new venues available for podcast experimentation is marketing. The specific content driven nature of podcast audience singles out particular markets simply based on the type of media that a listener is subscribing to. For example, a company that sells vintage car parts can immediately connect with their specific group of consumers by sponsoring podcasts about vintage cars, or even better, begin to produce their own podcast on the subject.

How are podcasts able to support branding efforts? First off, podcasts have already weeded out a specific, targeted marketing group. Offering an informative podcast helps establish within the consumer market a reputation as an expert in the field or as the leader in the industry. This then allows you to promote a product, service or general brand to the specific market your podcast listeners represent.

As far as advertising is concerned. Make sure to intrigue your audience with the advertisements, to do this make sure the advert has relevance to the show topic. For example; placing an advert for a fashion store on a show that is about cars won't intrigue your audience, because that isn't why their listening to your show, they want to hear about car related items - not fashion! This is where targeted marketing comes in. If your show is about cars, then place an advert which is related to cars! Not only will it seem less of an advert, but it may actually be of interest to your listener!

Coca-Cola

Coca-Cola have taken advantage of podcasts by offering a series of podcasts on their site covering different areas of their beverages. Such as "why we love sweet tastes", "the science of taste" etc. These are great for promoting products, as they make the product seem more appealing. However, this type/style of informercial podcast limits the amount of episodes you can produce, as their is only so much you can cover with this type of information, as it isn't updating, and the information isn't changing, so there is never a need to update the episodes, or create new ones.

Of course, you don't have to use podcasts solely for this purpose, for example; if you're a real estate business; you can of course create episodes explaining how your company works, how real estate works, what makes you stand out from the crowd etc. But you can also make it "current" by talking about the current properties for sale, talking about them, and maybe even what you like about them. Not only is this advertisement for your brand, but also your service and products.

Podcasting for Businesses

Education

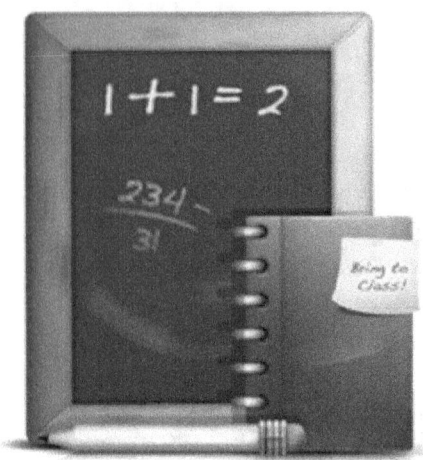

One market that has embraced podcasting with open arms is education and academia. Podcasts have been employed in a variety of ways by many universities and institutions. The opportunities with podcasts are seemingly endless in an environment where lectures and lessons are key to disseminating information.

The success of podcasts in universities and colleges is comparable to training in the business world. The dissemination of information through podcasting allows for a variety of resources to be sought out and shared throughout a corporation. Many companies are favoring podcasting as a training tool in the corporate world. These businesses are finding that podcasts are an essential and incredibly useful tool.

Business to Customer

Podcasting is finding it's niche in business to customer commerce. Podcasting offers the opportunity to break into new markets. Business to Customer marketing is ripe with the chance to win over new customers. Virgin Atlantic, for example have developed podcasts as travel guides for the destinations available on Virgin Atlantic Flights. Business to Customer podcasting is directed at reaching not only deeper into the existing market, but searching for those who haven't yet discovered your business which should offer something they want. It also takes away the feel of a huge corporation and makes it seem more personal to your consumer, giving it that unique touch.

Business to Business

Podcasts are proving useful in reaching new markets as well. A typical business to business podcast usually involves interviews with the "rock stars" or "leaders" of an industry. The average business to business subscriber is looking for insight and tips, perhaps they want to learn why your company's product line is better suited for their business, or what the latest industry trends and thinking are in a particular sector. Regardless, the content you include in your podcast will determine the type of markets you reach. Podcasts are also useful in establishing a presence and credibility in your field. Podcasting to a business to business audience does not mean that you have to divulge industry secrets, but sharing tidbits of information which will in turn, draw attention.

Build a Library of Content

Another reason for starting a podcast is that it allows for you and your business to build a library of content which will allow your customers and audience to go back and listen to. The sooner you start your podcast, the more content there will be in the archives for people to go back and listen to!

Podcasting for Businesses

Become a Market Leader

Having a podcast can establish you as an innovator and a pioneer in new communications, and also show that your company is not afraid to wait for everyone else to use new mediums to communicate with them. The media landscape has begun to shift in recent years from traditional mediums to social media like blogs, wikis and podcasting. Social media represents change in the playing field between businesses and consumers, corporations and individuals. It creates a dialogue like never before, and embracing podcasting demonstrates your organisation's willingness to participate in this dialogue. You can clearly establish that you are on the cutting edge of communications and are following the trends of consumer demand.

PR of Podcasting

Public Relations is incredibly important for businesses to connect with customers, and a podcast can add to your company's PR strategy. Every business, no matter the industry, can benefit from creating content that is interesting and educational to their target market. You are, in a very real sense, conducting your own PR campaign to promote yourself and your company in a positive light, your growing reputation of expertise will also help you get mentioned more in the press. Normally, reporters are not likely to call your company because they assume you'll simply want to pitch your products and services. However, as the host of your company podcast, you become more of a resource than a company representative

You can increase the speed at which you become well known as the "go to" person by doing press releases around special episodes of your podcast. Each listener you have is a potential customer that you are slowly gaining the trust of before you can ever make a sale.

By having a podcast, you can let your customers and audience have their say! Not only does it allow you to gain information from the general public on where they feel your company is striving, but it also allows you to find out where they feel your company could improve.

It also allows potential customers to see the strong relationship you have with your customers, which will in turn give them more confidence in your company and will separate you from the crowd.

The Future

Chapter Summary

In this chapter we will be taking a look at the future of your podcast. What do you when you have all of the initial steps completed.

What can you do you keep your podcast current? What are your future plans for your podcast? There are a few things you want to think about to keep a direction to your podcast.

Summary

Let's assume that time travel has not yet been invented so you need to think of ways in which your show will evolve in both the near and the distant future. You have already done the hard part which is setting up and establishing your show but the next challenge is keeping it current and coming up with new ideas to keep your podcast at the top of the board.

The Future

First we'll take a look at the near future. Near future meaning the coming weeks and months. What will you be doing next week to keep your show current? How about the week or the month after that?

If your show is a news show then you could think about introducing a new segment to your show, this could be anything from an interesting or funny piece of news you found or even an interview with someone. Adding a new segment to your show can really help keep things going and it will change it up so as to keep the listener interested in your podcast.

Never settle, always be looking for new ideas for your podcast. Is there something you feel that you were not happy with on your last show and you think you can improve on for your next episode? There are always things to improve on, they may be the smallest thing to your listener but to you it may be a big deal. Anything that helps you gain confidence in doing your show is always a plus. Never stop tweaking, don't be afraid to change your show up every so often because at the end of the day it's your show and you can do what you please with it, always remember to ask your audience what they feel you could improve on, they may come up with something you didn't think of.

A lot of people will try to reduce the 'uhhs' and 'umms', and this is a good thing to reduce, it is also something that we do naturally. You can replace these with just silence if you like and remember that most of the time silence will be more awkward for you to be in than it is for your listener to listen to.

Planning for the near future can also include planning for guests and giveaways. Plan when you are next going to get a guest on your show in advance so that you can be guaranteed a time slot with them. If you don't plan in advance people may have plans on the day or time that you are available. If you plan in advance then you can both plan around it.

Did you know?

Time travel has not yet been invented, so we found it difficult to pop to the future and grab a fact.

The Future

This has been looked at in previous chapters as a way of engaging your listeners or viewers. Giveaways. You may want to run a giveaway (or competition) on your podcast in the near future as it's something that you can easily do quickly, it doesn't require a lot of planning and gives back to your audience.

This next point is for both the near and distant future which is milestones. Milestones are goals that you can set for yourself personally and for your show. These may be milestones you want to reach downloads wise, or a millstone you want to reach episode wise. You should always set yourself goals not only in real life but also on your show as it gives you something to aim for and will give you a great sense of achievement when you reach that goal. You should never stop aiming for something, set your self goals that you think you can easily achieve and also some that you think will require more work and that are harder to reach or more ambitious.

The Distant Future
If you reach a significant number of episodes and you think it is something that you will carry on then you will need to set out some future goals. You cannot plan for every possibility but there are somethings you can plan for. Depending on the rate of growth and age of your show you can set out a target for when you think you would like to get advertisers or sponsors (if you do at all) on board. Obviously the quicker the rate of growth and the older the show, the sooner you can look for sponsors.

If you are a business you can lay out different campaigns and when they are going to start and finish. You can set the goals for what you want to have achieved by the end of these campaigns. When you are using podcasting to help your business you need to plan for both the near and distant future with detail.

Never stray away from your original core audience, they are the people that helped to make your show what it is or what it will become, so the worst thing you can do is to start to alienate them or ignore them. That really goes as a rule in general in which you should never alienate or forget your audience as without them your show may not become what you want it to become.

You may have hiccups along the way but if it is something you truly want to continue you won't give up on it. Just because the numbers may not be great one week or unexpected problems arise does not meant that there are not people out there who love your show, in the end it's up to you whether you want thousands of listeners or viewers or if you want a few that you can really get to know and talk to. Of course, having lots of subscribers is not a bad thing, quite the contrary, but it is a lot easier to get to know less rather than more.

We wish you all the best in the future for your podcast and hope that you continue with your new hobby, or even job! We also hope that this book has been an essential and useful tool in helping you setup, improve or evaluate your podcast.

Glossary

Advertising IO - Form used to allow companies or individuals to buy advertising. Includes information about the advertisement.
CBR - Constant Bitrate.
CPM (Cost Per Mile) - Reflects the cost per 1000 estimated views of the ad.
CPR (Cost Per Rating) - Method of comparing different media forms by relating costs of advertising units to audience ratings.
Clipping - Distortion when an amplifier is overdriven and attempts to deliver an output voltage beyond it's maximum capability.
Compression - Reducing the dynamic range within sound.
DNS - Domain Name Servers.
Database - Holds all the information to do with your website.
Download - Copying data from one computer (or server) to another.
Dynamic Range - The range of loud and soft volumes of sound occurring.
EQ - Boost or cut certain frequencies.
FX - Unusual effects.
Feed Validator - Used to make sure an RSS feed has no errors.
File Size - The measure of the size of a computer file. Normally measured in bytes with a prefix, such as "kilo", "mega" and "giga".
Format - A particular way information is encoded for storage in a computer file.
Gain - The amount of "boost" applied to a channel.
HDMI (High-Definition Multimedia Interface) - Compact audio/video interface for transmitting uncompressed digital data.
Hot Shoe - A socket on a camera with direct electrical contacts for an attached flashgun or other accessory.
ID3 Tag - Metadata container most often used with the MP3 audio file format. Allows information such as the title, artist, album and artwork.
Input - Data or signals put into a system, or computer.
Interference (Noise) - An unpleasant sound unintentionally added to a desired sound. Normally caused by other audio cables, or electrical cables.
MP3 - A means of compressing a sound sequence into a very small file.
Mix Minus - Output to a certain device which contains everything except the input from that device.
Monetisation - Making something profitable.
Output - Produce, deliver or supply using a computer or other device.
Overhead - The expense of a certain operation.

Pan - Sending the audio signal to either the centre, left or right channel.
Peaks - The highest audio level.
Plosive - Denoting a consonant that is produced by stopping the airflow using the lips, teeth or palate, followed by a sudden release of air. Such as; *t, k, p, d, g* and *b*.
Podcast - A multiple digital file made available on the Internet for downloading to a portable media player, computer etc.
Podcatching Software - A computer application used to download various media via an RSS or XML feed.
Post-production - A term used for all stages after the end of recording of the completed work.
Pre-production - Preparing all the elements involved in a podcast, or other performance.
RSS (Rich Site Summary) - A standardised system for distribution of content.
Referral - Referring from one thing/place to another.
Rendering - The process of creating temporary video and audio render files that can't be played in realtime.
SDI - Dedicated digital video interface used to carry broadcast quality video content.
Sample rate - Defines the number of samples per second taken from a continuous signal to make a discrete signal.
Streaming - A method of relaying data over a computer network as steady, continuous stream allowing playback to proceed while subsequent data is being received.
Subscribe - Arrange to receive something regularly.
VU (Volume Unit) Meter - A visual display of the loudness of a signal.
Volume - How loud or soft the final output of a specific channel (or multiple channels) is.
WAV (Waveform Audio File Format) - File format standard for storing an audio bitstream on computers.
Waveform - A curve showing the shape of a wave at a given time.
Wavelength - The distance between successive crests of a wave.
XML - A metalanguage that allows users to define their own customised markup language, especially to display documents on the Internet.
dB (Decibels) - A unit used to measure the intensity of a sound.

Cheat Sheet

Website Hosting

Host	Website
Godaddy	godaddy.com
BlueHost	bluehost.com
HostGator	hostgator.com

Podcast Hosting

Host	Website
Blip	blip.tv
Libsyn	libsyn.com
Amazon S3	aws.amazon.com/s3

Audio Editing Software

Software	Website	Platform
Audacity	audacity.sourceforge.net	Mac, PC
Adobe Audition	adobe.com/products/audition	Mac, PC
GarageBand	apple.com/garageband	Mac

WordPress Themes

Name	Website
WooThemes	woothemes.com
WPZoom	wpzoom.com
Templatic	templatic.com

Podcast Jingle's

Name	Website
Music Bakery	musicbakery.com
Incompetech	incompetech.com
Megatrax	megatrax.com

Video Editing Software

Software	Website	Platform
Final Cut Pro X	apple.com/finalcut	Mac
iMovie	apple.com/imovie	Mac
Sony Vegas	sonycreativesoftware.com/vegassoftware	PC
Wirecast	telestream.net/wire-cast/overview.htm	Mac, PC

Content Management Systems

Name	Website
Wordpress	wordpress.org
Drupal	drupal.org
Joomla	joomla.org

Export Settings

Format - MP3

Sample Type - 44,100Hz Mono

Format Settings - 64Kbps CBR (Constant Bit Rate)

PodcastAssist
Find more help at **PodcastAssist.com**